"This new collection of essays on an exemplary group of Catholic writers, all women, includes many of the most distinguished authors of the early-twentieth-century literary revival and some of our greatest contemporaries. The richest of touchstones, it gives some of our day's finest writers and scholars the chance to lead us on a journey of rediscovery. Readers will find terrific introductions to established greats such as Undset, Spark, and Godden as well as some of the first explorations of the theological depths of contemporaries such as Morrison, McDermott, and Tartt. What a perfectly imagined, timely, and exciting book."

—**James Matthew Wilson**, author of *Saint Thomas and the Forbidden Birds*

"When *Women of the Catholic Imagination: Twelve Inspired Novelists You Should Know* arrived in my inbox, I was pleasantly surprised to find that all twelve of the women writers featured are future considerations for Well-Read Mom selections. This treasured resource will acquaint readers with literary gems that are waiting to be discovered once again."

—**Marcie Stokman**, president and founder of Well-Read Mom

"A terrific volume that demonstrates the way Catholicism has informed and in turn been enriched by the imaginative works of a number of female authors, most of whom have been unduly neglected. Correcting that injustice, these elegantly written essays invite readers to explore texts that deepen our appreciation of the great mysteries of human life: good and evil, despair and hope, tragedy and redemption."

—**Thomas Hibbs**, J. Newton Rayzor Sr. Professor of Philosophy and Dean Emeritus, Baylor University

"Each essay in this book beams a light on a Catholic luminary who may have been overshadowed by her male contemporaries. Now, thanks to this book, the brilliant women of the Catholic imagination shine forth. Reading this collection not only introduces you to more friends in the Church but also extends your reading list!"

—**Jessica Hooten Wilson**, author of *Flannery O'Connor's "Why Do the Heathen Rage?" A Behind-the-Scenes Look at a Work in Progress*

"This exciting collection of essays on the life and work of Catholic female literary figures calls out not only to Roman Catholic readers but to those who are interested in the way that literature can evoke those truths we find it difficult to speak about without the help of story, and the legacy of women throughout history who have done just that."

—**Joy Clarkson**, author of *Aggressively Happy* and *You Are a Tree*

WOMEN
of the CATHOLIC
IMAGINATION

WOMEN
of the CATHOLIC
IMAGINATION

TWELVE INSPIRED NOVELISTS
YOU SHOULD KNOW

EDITED BY *Haley Stewart*

Published by Word on Fire,
Elk Grove Village, IL 60007
© 2024 by Word on Fire Catholic Ministries
Printed in the United States of America
All rights reserved

Cover design, typesetting, and interior art direction
by Rozann Lee, Clare Sheaf, and Cassie Bielak

ISBN: 978-1-68578-096-8

Library of Congress Control Number: 2023952249

Contents

A Good Novel
Can Change Your Life

Haley Stewart

A good novel can change your life. It has happened to me.

I sat on a blanket in my backyard reading the last fifty pages of Evelyn Waugh's *Brideshead Revisited* on a spring evening. It was my senior year at the world's largest Baptist university, and I wept with joy as I encountered the power of the sacraments of the Catholic Church for the first time. It wasn't because the book *explained* the sacraments clearly. In fact, the Catholic characters' understanding of theology in the novel is quite muddled. They cannot effectively explain to Charles, the agnostic protagonist, *why* Last Rites (Anointing of the Sick) would be necessary. But as Charles watches, transfixed, as a lapsed Catholic character makes the sign of the cross on his deathbed, accepting the extraordinary salvific grace of the sacrament offered to him by an ordinary parish priest, I was overcome with longing for that same sacramental grace. Had it been simply explained to me instead of offered in a story, I may never have understood at all. Two years later, my husband and I were receiving the sacraments of Reconciliation, First Holy Communion, and Confirmation at our local Catholic parish.

My husband was pushed across the Tiber not by *Brideshead Revisited* but through the works of American Catholic writer Flannery O'Connor (featured in this collection of essays). Catholic faith "clicked" for him with a steady ingestion of the shocking short stories and disturbing Southern gothic novels by this famous authoress of Milledgeville, Georgia. Years after our conversion, I took something of a literary pilgrimage to Andalusia, the family home of O'Connor. I walked around the house and watched the peacocks, descendants of her beloved flock, wander around their coop. I rocked in a chair on her front porch, awestruck that I was on the same porch where she sat, her mind humming with stories that changed our lives.

Waugh and O'Connor are novelists you might find high-lighted in any course on Catholic novels, likely accompanied by G.K. Chesterton, Graham Greene, and Walker Percy. But they're certainly not the only worthwhile Catholic novelists. As I sought out other writers as a new Catholic, I kept discovering more and more gems. I picked up a one-thousand-page book by twentieth-century Norwegian author Sigrid Undset (featured in this collection). As I stepped into the medieval Norway of her masterpiece, the world of the protagonist Kristin Lavransdatter, Undset captivated me. When I learned that she converted to Catholicism soon after writing the three novels that make up the epic *Kristin Lavransdatter*, I was unsurprised. "How could she *not* have become Catholic after writing this?"

Kristin Lavransdatter is saturated with Catholicism—and not because Undset's characters are so very holy. Kristin is less a saint and more of a fourteenth-century Don Draper—driving the reader mad with frustration at her relentless mistakes and selfishness! But it is a Catholic story as *Brideshead Revisited* is Catholic: the Catholic characters are messy, broken, and confused, but the grace and mercy of God surrounds them, haunts them, and in turn haunts us, the readers.

A good Catholic novel can communicate truth about God, about sin, about grace, about sacrament. It can evangelize through one of the most powerful methods: *story*. As human beings, we are wired for story by our Creator. Jesus taught his disciples through parables, knowing his followers could not grasp those lessons as effectively any other way. We see this same phenomenon at other times in Holy Scripture. When the prophet Nathan confronts King David with the reality of his betrayal and murder of Uriah, he does not walk up to the king's throne and begin condemning his sin. Instead, he *tells a story*. He describes a rich man who takes the only beloved lamb of a poor neighbor. With Nathan's help, this powerful story is what reveals David to himself. He comes to understand that he is the evil man, the thief of a cherished lamb: Uriah's wife, Bathsheba.

We understand ourselves through stories. And if we want to evangelize the world, we must tell good stories. Novels speak to our hearts, and their characters journey with us for the rest of our lives. The very best books call us out of our comfort zones to conversion. They point us to what is true and good and beautiful and to their ultimate source: Truth, Goodness, and Beauty itself.

Over the years since my conversion, I've discovered more and more Catholic writers whose books have become friends. And brilliant Catholic women keep showing up to change my life with their novels. In addition to Flannery O'Connor, there is Josephine Ward, Caryll Houselander, Gertrud von le Fort, Caroline Gordon, Rumer Godden, Alice Thomas Ellis, Muriel Spark, Toni Morrison, Alice McDermott, and Donna Tartt—all of whom deserve more readers of their brilliant writing. Recent and still-living novelists included in this volume call into question the idea that the Catholic literary movement fizzled out after the era of Waugh and O'Connor.

In my eagerness to learn more about them, I looked for a volume introducing readers to Catholic women novelists, but I couldn't find one. While there are many titles lauding Catholic men like J.R.R. Tolkien, Walker Percy, Graham Greene, and Evelyn Waugh (and to be fair, O'Connor is often included in this pantheon of writers), many of the Catholic women have been forgotten over the decades (Caroline Gordon, for instance); or, if they are remembered, their Catholic identity has been largely unexplored (like Toni Morrison and Donna Tartt). I hope this book brings these writers and their Catholic faith into a much-deserved spotlight. They are simply too good not to share.

WHAT MAKES A NOVELIST A *CATHOLIC* NOVELIST?

Much ink has been spilt on what counts as a "Catholic novel." What makes a book a *Catholic* book? When determining which writers to include in this volume, we began with the most basic consideration: Is the writer a baptized Catholic? This measurement disqualified some wonderful non-Catholic writers like Willa Cather and Susannah Clarke, who offer a powerful sacramental worldview from their Protestant tradition. But there are plenty of Catholic women writers to explore—far too many, in fact, to include in this collection.

Pope Benedict XVI, speaking as Cardinal Ratzinger at the time, claimed, "The only really effective apologia for Christianity comes down to two arguments, namely the saints the Church has produced and the art which has grown in her womb."[1]

This art that has grown in the womb of the Church includes Catholic novels infused with a sacramental view that evangelizes the reader with beauty. These writers' imaginations have been formed by the sacred, and the worlds of their stories are permeated with grace—sometimes explicit grace, sometimes hidden grace. Their novels will challenge and convict. In some of their books, Catholicism is front and center. (You simply cannot get away from nuns in Godden's *In This House of Brede* or McDermott's

---

1. Joseph Ratzinger with Vittorio Messori, *The Ratzinger Report: An Exclusive Interview on the State of the Church*, trans. Salvator Attanasio and Graham Harrison (San Francisco: Ignatius, 1985), 129.

The Ninth Hour.) Others, like the works of Flannery O'Connor, are largely devoid of Catholic characters and settings. But as Catholic writers, their stories have been formed by their faith. And their breathtaking artistry has influenced the world. Their work is characterized by hope, even when their stories unsettle us with the darkness of violence, suffering, or doubt. The chaos of despair does not prevail. In Flannery O Connor's words, "The Catholic writer, insofar as he has the mind of the Church, will feel life from the standpoint of the central Christian mystery: that it has, for all its horror, been found by God to be worth dying for."[2]

And yet, while I know firsthand how a good Catholic novel can evangelize, I think most of the writers featured in this volume would have scoffed at the idea of setting out to write a book to convert their readers. Instead, the Catholic novelist is interested in crafting the best and truest story she can and leaving the rest up to the Holy Spirit.

It is also worth noting that none of the gifted writers in this volume are canonized saints, although some did live lives of inspiring personal holiness. Others celebrated in these essays may be controversial, with messy biographies and even complicated relationships with the Church. (Many had difficulty with the changes that followed Vatican II, for example. Others struggled with certain Catholic doctrines.) But if we used lack of scandal in a creative's life as the rubric for considering their work "Catholic" —if only flawless, respectable artists can apply—then we would certainly have to throw out some of the finest Catholic artists. We would miss out on Graham Greene's incredible novel *The Power and the Glory* and Caravaggio's stunning painting *The Conversion on the Way to Damascus*.

---

2. Flannery O'Connor, "The Church and the Fiction Writer," in *The Flannery O'Connor Collection* (Park Ridge, IL: Word on Fire Classics, 2019), 167.

WOMEN OF THE CATHOLIC IMAGINATION

The essays in this collection begin with Josephine Ward, who was born in 1864, and end with Donna Tartt, who was born in 1963. Their lives span over 150 years, from the American Civil War through the COVID-19 global pandemic. Some are American; others are English, Scottish, German, or Norwegian. There are twentieth-century American Catholic converts and members of English recusant families. Some are happily married; some are single mothers, divorcees, eccentrics, or mystics. In the essays that follow, you'll discover how these writers are connected to figures like Servant of God Dorothy Day, Edith Stein (St. Teresa Benedicta of the Cross), Frank Sheed, and St. Philip Howard. Pope Benedict XVI read the writing of Gertrud von le Fort. St. John Henry Newman corresponded with Josephine Ward about her work. The connections are fascinating.

These inspiring women defy easy labels. Alice Thomas Ellis wrote cookbooks as well as novels, and unapologetically smoked cigarettes and drank with her friends while critiquing modern feminism. Toni Morrison, a convert who loved the Traditional Latin Mass and grieved its loss, became the first Black woman and the only American Catholic woman to receive the Nobel Prize for literature. I sometimes wonder if the women featured in this volume would have gotten along very well together. Some espoused very traditional views, while others challenged them. They have strong personalities and differing opinions on various movements, although they do not fit neatly into ideological boxes. But they are all baptized Catholics and inspired novelists.

The writers explored in this book are gifted in myriad ways, but they are especially able to portray a depth of female characters rarely found in literature. Some achieve this by exploring the domestic sphere in a powerful way. Few stories examine the experience of womanhood and motherhood like *Kristin Lavransdatter*, for example, in which Undset presents the demands of marriage,

6

pregnancy, birth, breastfeeding, and raising children as a sacred space in which God moves through joy and through suffering. I've been told by priests who read this epic that Kristin Lavransdatter helped them in their pastoral ministry by offering them a richer understanding of marriage and motherhood.

These writers bring their feminine genius to the task of writing novels, but this does not mean that their works are only for women. They are for anyone ready to encounter good novels that form a sacramental imagination. They are for readers eager to be challenged by works of enduring beauty to wrestle with truth. They are for everyone interested in deep questions and in search of a good novel. And a good novel can change your life.

Haley Stewart is the Editor of Word on Fire's children's imprint. She is the author of *The Grace of Enough, Jane Austen's Genius Guide to Life*, and *The Sister Seraphina Mysteries*.

Josephine Ward:
Transforming a Heritage of Exile

Eleanor Bourg Nicholson

> We have to thank Mrs. Ward for a singularly interesting and
> stimulating novel, in which, though the Roman Catholic stand-
> point of the author is never concealed, anything savouring of
> aggressiveness or proselytism is scrupulously avoided.[1]

This review of Josephine Ward's 1906 *Out of Due Time*, which
appeared in a major weekly British publication, may strike today's
reader as scant praise. In fact, this is a remarkable statement,
capturing Ward's singular contribution to English Catholic
literature. This talented and popular novelist emerged from the
complicated heritage of English Catholicism to engage upon a
national scene. Alongside her husband, she served as a lynchpin
between the tumultuous nineteenth century and the flowering of
the English Catholic novel in the 1930s, boldly articulating to her
readers the complicated reality of being an "English Papist." Her
life united two critical threads of English Catholic identity: the
heritage of martyrs and recusants, and the intellectual vibrancy
of mid-Victorian conversion. This is represented in the patronage
of two shining lights of the faith in England in the modern era:

---

1. Review from *The Spectator*, included in the front of the 1906 edition of
Out of Due Time.

St. Philip Howard and St. John Henry Cardinal Newman, both of whom had a formative relationship with the novelist.

WARD'S RECUSANT LINEAGE

In the late sixteenth century, St. Philip Howard, the 13th Earl of Arundel and attainted Duke of Norfolk, suffered an eleven-year imprisonment in the Tower of London because he had returned to the faith. Queen Elizabeth I and her entourage sought to eradicate the papist taint among her subjects, declaring every act, ritual, or observance of Catholicism treasonous. She was able thereby to decree a bloody tidal wave of repressions and executions. Fearing, however, a strong negative public response if, after so much persecution and death, she ordered the execution of a high-ranking English peer, the queen commanded Philip Howard's imprisonment instead, until his death (of dysentery or of poison) in 1595.[2]

Since the slow martyrdom of St. Philip Howard, the Dukes of Norfolk have remained steadfastly recusant. In fact, this branch of the British peerage is unique in having maintained the faith since the sixteenth century. Within this heritage, there emerged a particular character of besieged English Catholicism, into which young Josephine Mary Hope, granddaughter of Henry Granville Fitzalan-Howard, 14th Duke of Norfolk, was born in 1864. The knowledge of the Elizabethan martyrs remained strong throughout Josephine's life; indeed, her final work was *Tudor Sunset*, an account of the last years of Elizabeth's reign. Ward wrote:

> I started preoccupied with the heroism of my forefathers in the Faith, and I found my heroes, on closer inspection, most wonderful and yet quite curiously companionable; I felt not only spiritual and blood-relationship, but to me the lovable traits

2. See Joseph Pearce, *Faith of Our Fathers: A History of True England* (San Francisco: Ignatius, 2022) for a full account of the ruthless ambitions of Queen Elizabeth I.

that are specifically English. They were never downhearted; they positively enjoyed ordinary hardships, and the smile of confidence and love provoked by adventure and peril would reappear between the torments of the rack, or in the sight of the butcher's knife that was to dismember the living bodies they had never greatly valued.[3]

The duke and his wife raised their children in accordance with a long-standing practice: the sons were raised according to the faith of their father, and the daughters as members of the Church of England. In the mid-Victorian period, however, the duchess and her daughters (including Josephine's mother) joined the ranks of converts. So too did the lawyer James Hope-Scott, Josephine's father, and William George Ward and his wife Frances, the parents of Josephine's future spouse. Josephine's parents both died by the time she was eight years old, and she and her sisters and brother were raised by their grandmother, then a widow and therefore the Dowager Duchess of Norfolk. The children would spend their formative years at Arundel Castle, the seat of the Duke of Norfolk, surrounded by the joint heritage of three hundred years of recusancy and the spirit of conversion that would so define mid-Victorian Catholicism. While the former element owed much to the patronage of St. Philip Howard, the latter would owe commensurately to the patronage of John Henry Newman.

NEWMAN AND WARD

Conversion was not to be lightly undertaken. Anti-Catholicism had received legislative sanction in 1534 when the Act of Uniformity forcibly united government and church. Subsequently, anti-Catholicism became a vital characteristic of true Englishness. By the nineteenth century, legislative change brought limited liberation. As England and her national Church struggled to

3. Josephine Ward, *Tudor Sunset* (London: Sheed and Ward, 1932), 10.

meet the challenges of science, empire, industrial and population growth, and the increasing of the political franchise, they also struggled with the ponderous question of the "priest-ridden" Irish. The result of this web of tension was Parliament's passing of a bill granting Catholic Emancipation, signed on April 16, 1829, by a weeping King George IV.

Catholic Emancipation was followed by an increase of abuse against the papists in the 1830s. As was frequently the case, anti-Catholic abuse prompted a counter-development. 1833 marked the beginning of the "Oxford" or "Tractarian" movement, involving a series of "Tracts for the Times" by leading "High Church" members of the Church of England (nearly all of them intimately associated with Oxford University). These Tracts argued for a revitalization of the Church, a return to ancient religious roots, an emphasis on tradition and the writings of the Church Fathers, High-Church ritualism and ceremony, and authority. The work of the Oxford Movement concluded in 1841 with John Henry Newman's notorious "Tract 90," which signaled catastrophe for Anglicanism and revitalization for the papists. This document, with its seeming endorsement of many points recognizable as Roman Catholic, prompted uproar and fury against the High Church faction. Public confidence in Newman and in the Tractarian movement evaporated in the "universal storm of indignation with which the Tract was received." Within four years, Newman entered the Catholic Church, and within two more years, he was ordained a priest of that Church.

A few weeks before Newman's conversion, one of his most eager disciples, William Ward, also converted. "Ideal" Ward, so-called because of his *The Ideal of the Christian Church*—which was as enthusiastically condemned as Tract 90—would go on to become one of the most dedicated and zealous of converts, an ultramontane theologian and philosopher famous for his extremist views on the question of papal infallibility, desiring "a Papal Bull every morning with his *Times* at breakfast."[4] The conversions continued apace, including the 1850 conversion of the wife and daughters of the Duke of Norfolk, noted above. In 1851, Newman delivered a series of lectures *On the Present Position of Catholics in England*. That same year, James Hope-Scott, Josephine's father, converted.

As Newman commented in *On the Present Position of Catholics in 1851*, Catholicism was "the victim of a prejudice which perpetuates itself and gives birth to what it feeds upon,"[5] a tradition pervading every point of culture, politics, and everyday life, "a tradition floating in the air."[6] Little wonder in this environment that one of the greatest temptations to recusant Catholics was to live as cloistered a life as possible, avoiding the hostile world outside the papist battlements. Long barred from participation in public life, they were content to remain where they were safe, and some viewed converts with marked suspicion. This is clearly shown in Josephine Ward's first published novel, *One Poor Scruple*. The central family of the novel identifies their home as a place of religious pilgrimage, a "Home of the Persecuted" separate from the rest of England.[7] "The persecuted had come, in many cases, to idealise the enforced seclusion and inaction of penal days."[8] English Catholics remained "so secluded and so inactive" and were "satisfied" in this situation, much to the frustration of proactive and assertive converts of the period.[9]

4. Maisie Ward, *The Wilfrid Wards and the Transition*, vol. 1, *The Nineteenth Century* (New York: Sheed and Ward, 1934), 8.

5. Quoted in E.R. Norman, *Anti-Catholicism in Victorian England* (New York: Barnes & Noble, 1968), 13–14.

6. John Henry Newman, *Lectures on the Present Position of Catholics in England: Addressed to the Brothers of the Oratory in the Summer of 1851* (London: Longmans, Green, and Co., 1893), 87–88.

7. Newman, 40.

8. Josephine Ward, *One Poor Scruple* (Washington, DC: The Catholic University of America Press, 2023), 39.

9. Ward, 42.

Such was not the attitude of Newman, nor of many who converted in that mid-century flood tide. The Newmanites represented a dramatic shift, establishing a strong population of engaged and intellectually respectable papists within the mainstream of English culture and public discourse. The English might eschew the Oxford Movement and resent Newman as a traitor, but they could not completely dismiss him. In his 1851 lectures, Newman called for a laity "not arrogant, not rash in speech, not disputatious, but men who know their religion, who enter into it, who know just where they stand, who know what they hold and what they do not, who know their creed so well that they can give an account of it, who know so much of history that they can defend it . . . an intelligent, well-instructed laity."[10]

Following the enthusiastic engagement of her father, James Hope-Scott, and the example of both Newman and Manning, Josephine Mary Hope-Scott lived out this call for "an intelligent, well-instructed laity." From an early age, she exhibited a commitment of both head and heart to the faith. Her literary talent was also apparent, as is shown by the response of the elderly Newman, to whom she showed an early fictional work in 1887. His response was one of the final letters written in his own hand. In it he sent strong encouragement and constructive criticism, including the note that "there is perhaps too much *direct* teaching and preaching in the Tale"—almost immediately followed by the reassurance: "If I was not pleased with your work, if I did not think it likely to do glory to God, if I did not love you and take an interest in you, I should not have written."[11]

DOMESTIC LIFE AND *ONE POOR SCRUPLE*

The promise Newman saw in Josephine would require some years yet to blossom. That same year she married Wilfrid Ward, and her

10. Newman, *Lectures on the Present Position of Catholics in England*, 390.
11. Ward, *The Wilfrid Wards and the Transition*, 1:152.

life became focused upon domestic matters and her husband's work. While Wilfrid as a young man followed uncertainly in his father's footsteps toward a more insular and extreme attitude to the faith, together with Josephine he would come to exemplify Newman's vision for the Catholic laity. Wilfrid went on to become one of the most significant English Catholic thinkers of his day. A remarkable essayist and biographer, his most notable works included biographies of his father, of Cardinal Nicholas Wiseman, and of John Henry Newman, as well as close studies of Catholicism in England, from the Oxford Movement into the monumental questions posed by modernism in the first decade of the twentieth century. Further, Ward's work as the editor of the *Dublin Review* from 1906 to 1915 oversaw the publication of articles by G.K. Chesterton, Hilaire Belloc, and Francis Thompson, all of whom became personal friends of the Wards.

In addition to her loving support of Wilfrid and her intimate engagement with him on all theological, political, and historical topics, Josephine's life was quickly filling with maternal duties. Five children came in quick succession: Mary Josephine (called Maisie), Wilfrid (known as "Boy"), Theresa, Herbert, and Leo (who would later become a priest). Her own writing continued slowly. Inspiration was rife; in their early marriage, the Wards lived primarily upon the Isle of Wight, with the poet Alfred Lord Tennyson as their near neighbor.

In 1893, Josephine published a biography of St. Anselm through the Catholic Truth Society's *The Catholic's Penny Library*. Six years later marked the publication of Ward's first novel, *One Poor Scruple*. In it, the historical situation of English Catholicism is subsumed into an examination of the personal heritage of sin represented in the fall and death of young George Riversdale, the former heir to the estate of Skipton-le-Grange. The fruits of his sin haunt his surviving relatives, especially his widow, Madge, and his sister Mary. As a widow and a lapsed Catholic, Madge struggles with the temptation to accept the proposal of a divorced man (a marriage that would fully alienate her from Catholicism), even as her devout sister-in-law recoils from a call to the religious life. Branded within and without by their allegiance to a Church defined as alien, these Catholics must navigate the reality of fin-de-siècle England and their inward souls. Success—and salvation—relies on the re-evaluation of self-identity and an embrace of the transformative power of sacramental grace, even within the complexities of modern life. Moving away from the stereotypically imposed conception of popery, the rising generation of English Catholics is forced to embrace the faith in a new and sincere way.

These nuances of conflict reflect another challenge that Ward's work clearly addresses. Josephine Ward's desire for an authentic English Catholic literature had little to no specific heritage on which to call. Maisie Ward notes this clearly:

> Throughout the Church, but especially in England, there was an unmistakable artistic impoverishment. Thus the English Catholic who wished to write had to look far back into the past to find his Catholic fellows. Josephine Ward, who wished to write novels, was in a still worse case. For the novel is a post-Reformation product and up to the nineties there was no sufficient body of Catholic novelists to break the ground for her.[12]

One Poor Scruple is unequivocally Catholic as well as a masterfully executed novel that well deserves the positive reception afforded to it by Catholic and non-Catholic readers alike. Additionally, its reception testifies to a change in public feeling toward Catholicism itself. Increased secularism made the late-Victorian English audience more tolerant of loathed popery. Once again, Maisie Ward captures the conundrum of tolerance without comprehension:

12. Ward, 1:380.

The clear philosophy of life out of which the Classical English novel had come was dead; a note of interrogation had taken its place. The public was more willing than its grandparents had been to listen to a Catholic, but was one stage further from understanding what a Catholic artist was trying to convey. The critical vocabulary of the day did not contain the terms for an analysis of the deepest meaning of *One Poor Scruple*. But if there was not full perception, the praise was unanimous.[13]

Such success was a delight to the young author, and she continued to write alongside her duties as wife and mother.

Josephine's work was momentarily checked in 1901 by the sudden death of her eldest son, "Boy," from influenza that turned to meningitis. In this tragedy, the family turned ever more earnestly to the faith for consolation. Grief would bring an added note of empathy to Ward's writing in the future.

WARD'S CONTINUING CAREER

One Poor Scruple was followed by *The Light Behind* (1903), a novel enmeshed in English politics, living out the principle Wilfrid and Josephine both embraced that English Catholics should be involved in every aspect of national life. Three years later, at the height of the Roman Catholic engagement with and battle against modernism, Josephine's *Out of Due Time* (1906) appeared. Ward's close relationship with Baron von Hügel (whose work stopped upon the brink of the modernist heresy) and their intimate concern for both intellectual rigor and orthodoxy pervade this work. *Out of Due Time* tells the story of the temptations of modernism, seducing a charismatic young Catholic thinker. The novel does not merely contain Catholic characters or themes among other aspects; the novel is a poignant expression of English Catholicism at a critical point in history. In a special way, it captures the

13. Ward, 1:381.

personal suffering of Wilfrid Ward, whose faithfulness to the Church in this time of intellectual turmoil alienated him from many friends and former colleagues.

While the plots and concerns of *Great Possessions* (1909) and *The Job Secretary* (1911) are less ostentatiously Catholic, Josephine's recurring themes of temptation, sin, and the operation of grace are inescapable throughout both of these novels. The same can be said of the later novels *Not Known Here* (1921) and *The Plague of His Own Heart* (1925).

Most remarkable in this group of novels, however, is *Horace Blake* (1913). In this work, Ward provides an intimate psychological exploration of conversion and a vision of the prodigal son from a new and fascinating angle. The eponymous character is a play-wright whose life has championed his own apostasy and frank atheism. At the end of his life and the beginning of the novel, however, he returns to the faith. He leaves behind him a wife and daughter, as well as an eager young disciple in the form of a journalist, who must unpack this radical shift. If this reversion is authentic and sincere, what does it signify for his life's work, to which the women in his family have dedicated themselves? If it is not, as they rather hope is the case, how can they cope with the emptiness of the gesture implied in the final days of his life?

LOSS AND DEEPENING FAITH

After *Horace Blake*, Josephine Ward's attention shifted for some time. Wilfrid's health was failing, and his death in 1916 left her bereft, once again turning for solace to the faith that sustained her throughout her life, as well as to the loving support of her children. Together with her eldest daughter, Maisie, Josephine embarked on the task of editing and publishing Wilfrid's final papers and lectures.

In addition to the distress of the loss of her husband, Josephine faced the tumult and "mental disintegration" that came as a result of the First World War. Her children and grand-children remained a primary concern, but she was distressed by the changing world, which contracted on a personal level with age and loss and seemed increasingly incoherent on a societal level. Her discouragement with civilization fueled her interest in "the great question of Mussolini,"[14] culminating in her fictional portrait of the twentieth-century Italian dictator: *The Shadow of Mussolini* (1927). This novel, Maisie averred, "showed that at any rate there was an ideal alive in Italy. Mussolini might be wrong, he certainly was not futile." [15]

To the discouragement, disintegration, and fragmentation of the post-war world, Josephine could only find one answer: that of faith. Thus, after the First World War, Josephine and Maisie became involved in the Catholic Evidence Guild, which was established in 1918 with the intention of presenting Catholic teaching to the populace through open meetings and street preaching. Maisie wrote later of her mother's bravery in standing upon platforms in London parks, dressed in her traditional widow's weeds, and speaking to an often hostile audience on such topics as "Our Lady," "The Supernatural Life," and "Christian Marriage"—to the shock of aristocratic acquaintances who sometimes recognized her.

Their work for the guild produced further fruit, both familial and literary. Maisie met her future husband, the Australian lawyer and burgeoning Catholic thinker Frank Sheed. With Josephine's encouragement and the help of Leo Ward, the youngest of the Ward sons, Maisie and Frank established the Catholic publishing house Sheed and Ward.

The final years of Josephine's life continued her service and engagement with the world:

14. Maisie Ward, *The Wilfrid Wards and the Transition*, vol. 2, *Insurrection versus Resurrection* (London: Sheed and Ward, 1937), 521.

15. Ward, 2:522.

In her little Kensington home there came together the most varied assortment of human beings, all seeking and all finding. It seemed almost in her later years as though, like the hermits of old, when she withdrew a little, the world followed her.[16]

Family, friends, converts, priests, authors, poets, aristocrats—innumerable people came to her for counsel and guidance. Her instincts remained ever literary, as is captured in this little scene described by her granddaughter Rosemary Middleton:

> My Aunt Tetta was on the train in France with her mother and they passed a crumbling sort of chateau, obviously needing money spent on it. There was also a fairly new tennis court, though also sadly neglected. Granny commented rather dreamily that they must have built the tennis court in the hope of keeping the eldest son at home, but that, alas, it evidently hadn't worked. Tetta felt that perhaps only a novelist would instantly produce such an interesting interpretation.[17]

Ward's final novel, *Tudor Sunset*, was published in 1932, a year before her death. This fictional chronicle of the last years of the life of Elizabeth I provides a fascinating counterpoint to the better-known 1912 *Come Rack! Come Rope!* by Robert Hugh Benson. Without minimizing the bloody destruction wrought by "Good Queen Bess," Ward's compassionate approach to the blood-thirsty Tudor queen echoes the affectionate respect her saintly forebearer, St. Philip Howard, accorded the queen. The novel brings together the themes that had absorbed Ward throughout her life, especially Catholic identity and its relationship to patriotism and her conviction of the operation of grace. Her husband experienced a great deal of pain during "the Modernist controversy," because "it was not to him a sectarian controversy,

16. Ward, 2:532.

17. Author's personal correspondence.

but the vast question of the religious future of the human race." In a similar way, Josephine's concern for the operation of grace in the soul of Elizabeth I demonstrates her recognition that it was a vast question of the religious future of her nation and, even more critically, of a human soul.

The operation of grace, evinced in the life of the two saintly patrons of Josephine Ward and throughout her own life, remains the central point of her work and the key to her brilliance as a Catholic novelist, as well as her admirable qualities as a Catholic woman. Josephine had at one time intended to call her final novel *But One Death*, a reference to the words of St. Philip Howard. When the queen told him he had but to recant the faith to be restored to her favor, he replied, "Tell Her Majesty if my religion be the cause for which I suffer, sorry I am that I have but one life to lose."[18] The inscription he carved into the stone of his prison is still visible in the Tower of London: "Quanto plus afflicionis pro Christo in hoc saeculo, tanto plus gloriae cum Christo in futuro"—"The more affliction we endure for Christ in this world, the more glory we shall obtain with Christ in the next."[19] Josephine turned to these examples because, as her daughter attested, her "own secret" was that she greatly feared death.[20] This final novel serves as a personal prayer, in addition to the national prayer of the pious English Catholic, demonstrative of the heart of Christian hope:

Death in *Tudor Sunset* was not merely a peaceful passing; it was not only an offering for the soul of a nation and forgiveness of all enemies, it was, too, a triumph, a great bit of good news, a

18. Basil Hume, Homily given on the fourth centenary of St. Philip Howard's martyrdom, Arundel Cathedral, October 25, 1995, quoted in Pearce, *Faith of Our Fathers*, 193.

19. *The Life of St. Philip Howard*, from a manuscript at Arundel Castle, edited by Henry Grenville, 14th Duke of Norfolk, in 1857 (Chichester: Phillimore & Co., 1971), 50.

20. Ward, *The Wilfrid Wards and the Transition*, 2:535.

fulfilling of joy. And it was all this because the martyrs partook of the Sacrifice of Christ.[21]

As the first rumblings of the book's success began to be audible, Josephine Ward quietly passed from this life, leaving behind a literary legacy to which more widespread attention is long overdue.

RECOMMENDED READING

Josephine Ward. *Horace Blake.*
_____. *One Poor Scruple.*
_____. *Out of Due Time.*
_____. *Tudor Sunset.*
Maisie Ward. *The Wilfrid Wards and the Transition.* 2 volumes.

Eleanor Bourg Nicholson is a novelist, scholar, and homeschooling mother based in Charlottesville, Virginia. She counts Josephine Ward and St. Philip Howard as two of her dearest spiritual and artistic patrons.

---

21. Ward, 2:536.

Sigrid Undset: Novelist of Mercy

Amy Fahey

THREE SCANDALS

The life of the Norwegian novelist Sigrid Undset (1882–1949), author of the vast and beautiful portrait of a soul *Kristin Lavransdatter*, was marked early on by a series of scandals.

"I have been unfaithful to my husband." The opening line of Undset's early novella *Marta Oulie* (1907) shocked Norwegian society, treating marital infidelity with a matter-of-fact abruptness more characteristic of an Icelandic saga than an Edwardian novel. Undset was twenty-five, unmarried, and an agnostic when she published *Marta Oulie* and introduced readers to the theme of female self-determination that came to dominate her early fiction. Yet the novella also has a confessional quality—it is written as a series of diary entries expressing by turns passion, determination, confusion, doubt, ennui, and regret—revealing Undset's early preoccupation with the interior fallout from one's moral choices. The tension in *Marta Oulie* between the idealistic and unfettered pursuit of one's own desires and the inevitable confrontation with the consequences of those actions sets the stage for Undset's life and writings.

Not long after publishing *Marta Oulie*, Undset again af-
fronted the Norwegian public, this time by enacting a scenario
uncomfortably similar to those depicted in her early fiction. In
1909, she began an affair with the married Norwegian artist
Anders Svarstad, a man twelve years her senior, after meeting
him while on a travel fellowship in Rome. Svarstad already had
three children with his wife, Undset's childhood friend, Ragna
Moe. They attempted to keep the illicit relationship secret, but
when Sigrid became pregnant with Svarstad's child, he divorced
Ragna and the two were married. Undset and Svarstad had three
children together (including a severely mentally disabled daughter, Maren or "Mosse"), and their tumultuous union continued for
over a decade. During that time, Undset's literary fame increased,
and with the publication of *Kristin Lavransdatter* in 1922, her
international reputation as a novelist was secured.

By 1924, however, her marriage had collapsed and was formally
dissolved. In that same year, Undset caused the greatest of all
scandals: she converted to Catholicism. Prior to her conversion,
the best Undset could say for Catholicism was that it "has at least
form and is not irritating to one's intelligence."[1] It is thus difficult
to conceive what a shocking move her conversion was to Norwegian society, particularly to the artistic and clerical intelligentsia.
When Undset converted, Lutheranism had long been the state
religion; Catholic religious orders were not even allowed back
into the country until 1897, when Undset was fifteen. Catholics
remained a small fraction of the population—numbering less
than three thousand souls—and anti-Catholic sentiment ran
deep. Among prominent Norwegian artists, socialism and liber-
alism were the order of the day. But all of that changed with the
conversion of Norway's greatest female writer. As Dom Haakon
Bergwitz, pro-vicar of Oslo and a fellow convert, wrote shortly
after Undset's death, "Sigrid Undset's writings gave the Catholic

---

1. A.M. Scarre, "Sigrid Undset, T.O.S.D. 1882–1949," *Life of the Spirit
(1946–1964)* 4, no. 38 (1949): 70.

Church great prestige in Norway," acting as a "powerful weapon against the materialistic spirit of the times."[2]

How did Sigrid Undset—who once said of marriage that it "makes women stupid, or they dilute their demands on life, on their husband, and on themselves so much that they can scarcely be counted as human"—come to be such a powerful defender of the family in an age of social disintegration? And how could a woman who once said "I would personally prefer anything to marriage and motherhood as an occupation"[3] not only raise six children (two with severe mental disabilities)[4] but write so lyrically about her titular character Kristin, whose life is arguably defined—and spiritually refined—by marriage and motherhood? The answer is the same as it is for the fictional Kristin: God had been patiently waiting to redeem her misguided passion and idealism, to direct her gaze away from the self toward the "love which moves the sun and other stars"—in short, to thaw her Northern heart.

It is not an exaggeration to say that Undset first read, and then wrote, her way into the Church. The young Sigrid started out as self-willed and idealistic as her female protagonists. Her father, prominent Norwegian archaeologist Ingvald Undset, died when she was only eleven; she soon grew tired of formal schooling and, after a short secretarial course, spent nearly a decade as an office assistant in Christiania (modern-day Oslo). Here she observed firsthand the boredom and atomizing individualism of post-Christian Norway, all the while craving something more. She wrote to her friend Dea in 1902, "Don't get married unless

2. Haakon Bergwitz, "Despite Small Numbers, Catholicism in Norway Exerts Strong Influence," *The St. Louis Register,* June 14, 1950. Dom Bergwitz was also a Norwegian convert, entering the Church the same year as Undset.

3. Sigrid Undset, "Some Reflections on the Suffragette Movement," trans. Astrid O'Brien, in *Sigrid Undset: On Saints and Sinners,* ed. Deal Hudson, Wethersfield Institute, vol. 6 (San Francisco: Ignatius, 1993), 200.

4. After learning that Svarstad's ex-wife had placed her three children in an orphanage, Undset took them in and cared for them alongside her own three children.

you're so in love that you would rather be with your sweetheart in Hell than alone in Heaven."[5] She continued, "Even in happy marriages—I assume that they do exist, although I haven't seen any that I would call happy—happiness is assuredly paid for with one's most precious possessions."[6] Throughout these years of thinking about and observing flawed human relationships, she continued to nurture a fascination with medieval Scandinavia that her father had fostered early in her life. She carefully absorbed everything she could lay her hands on to help her enter more imaginatively into the struggles and passions of those who lived during that tumultuous yet spiritually compelling era. She had read the masterful *Njal's Saga* when she was ten; she now read the Danish ballads, tales of love and betrayal, and the writings of St. Birgitta of Sweden, whose visions of hell are so horrifying they arguably surpass those of Dante. She immersed herself in the lives and writings not only of Norway's great medieval saints—St. Olav, St. Sunniva, St. Hallvard, and others—but also of the English martyrs, the great Catherine of Siena, even the Catalan mystic Bl. Ramon Llull.

In the reality of the communion of the saints—so alien to modern Lutheran Norway—she began to find the satisfaction of her desire for relationships so intense they could draw her out of her own self-will. As she would later write in recounting her conversion, "The homage paid to the saints, fostered by the Church from the beginning, really seems to answer an ineradicable need of our nature."[7] She saw her embrace of Catholicism as the logical fruit of the choice between what Tolkien had earlier identified as the *goðlauss* (godless) strain of the Norse—"reliance upon self

5. Sigrid Undset, quoted in *The Unknown Sigrid Undset*, ed. Tim Page, trans. Tiina Nunnally (South Royalton, VT: Steerforth, 2001), 375.

6. Undset, 375.

7. Sigrid Undset, "Beyond Human Limitations," in *Through Hundred Gates: by Noted Converts from Twenty-Two Lands*, trans. Severin and Stephen Lamping (Milwaukee, WI: Bruce, 1940), 163.

and upon indomitable will"[8]—and trust in Christ, his Blessed Mother, and the saints: "It is for [man] to decide whether he will isolate himself in the hell of his own egotism, or give himself wholly to God and be freed of the limitations of self-love to go on to eternal possibilities."[9] No wonder, then, that she converted not long after writing *Kristin Lavransdatter*, and that one of her first undertakings as a Catholic was to translate Robert Hugh Benson's *The Friendship of Christ* into Norwegian.

TAMING THE FIRES OF SELF-LOVE

Though Undset had written several acclaimed modern novels, it was the publication of *Kristin Lavransdatter*, a trilogy set in fourteenth-century Norway, that earned her the Nobel Prize for Literature in 1928 (a medieval tetralogy, *The Master of Hestviken*— equally masterful and deserving of its own essay—followed in the years between 1925 and 1927). Admittedly, reading *Kristin Lavransdatter*—much like reading Lampeduza's *The Leopard*, Girondelle's *The Cypresses Believe in God*, Manzoni's *The Betrothed*, or any other thick Catholic novel—is a commitment. Catholic Worker founder Dorothy Day, a fellow convert who befriended Undset in her later years, recalls her own introduction to Kristin: "It was in 1926 or thereabouts that I first saw it, in the hands of my friend Freda, who lived next door. While she was reading it, her beach house remained unswept, her husband and son unfed. . . . As the years passed, I recommended it to all the women in the Catholic Worker movement, and they were spellbound by it too."[10] Such accounts of the novel's captivating effect have become almost commonplace among Catholic book groups and blogs

8. J.R.R. Tolkien, "Introduction to the Elder Edda," in *The Legend of Sigurd and Gudrun*, ed. Christopher Tolkien (New York: Houghton Mifflin, 2009), 24.

9. Undset, "Beyond Human Limitations," 162.

10. Dorothy Day, "On Pilgrimage," *The Catholic Worker*, November 1, 1977, https://catholicworker.org/582-html/.

today, as the novel enjoys a deservedly renewed popularity among Catholics in our own age.

The opening sentence of *Kristin* could not be more radically removed from the world of *Marta Oulie*: "When the earthly goods of Ivar Gjesling the Younger of Sundbu were divided up in the year 1306, his property at Sil was given to his daughter Ragnfrid and her husband Lavrans Bjorgulfson."[11] After its saga-like opening, the novel introduces us to young Kristin, daughter of the saintly Lavrans and the moody, melancholic Ragnfrid, and proceeds to trace her entire life in a manner that combines the spare, stark tenor of an Icelandic saga with the psychological realism and descriptive richness of the modern novel. The result is, paradoxically, a novel that speaks intimately to each reader precisely *because* it is set in a time and place so seemingly removed from our own. Kristin lives in a world where the reality of the supernatural—both heathen and Christian—is assumed, and the reader is thus able to enter into Kristin's external and interior struggles without having to directly acknowledge the modern burden of unbelief.

It would be unfair to both author and reader to attempt to summarize a novel with such a vast scope and intricate design. One could dedicate the better part of a lifetime to tracing various themes and tensions in the novel—marriage, family, fatherhood, motherhood, sin, redemption, shame, mercy, intercession, manliness, womanliness, obligations, passions, man, nature and the supernatural, and so many others—as well as to appreciating the novel as a work of art. The major events of the novel occur in particular seasons, both natural and liturgical, for a reason; the stories of the saints whose feasts are being commemorated interweave beautifully with the narrative timeline, and the natural world provides a rich commentary upon the story. When Kristin undertakes a battle of wills with her saintly father, Lavrans,

11. Sigrid Undset, *Kristin Lavransdatter*, trans. Tiina Nunnally (New York: Penguin, 1997), 5.

wishing to compel him to release her from her betrothal to Simon so that she will be free to marry Erlend, whose paramour she has become, the "iciness" between father and daughter is mirrored in nature:

> For those who were waiting for the redemption of spring, it seemed as if it would never come. The days grew long and bright, and the valley lay in a haze of thawing snow while the sun shone. But frost was still in the air, and the heat had no power. At night it froze hard; great cracking sounds came from the ice, a rumbling issued from the mountains, and the wolves howled and the foxes yipped all the way down in the village, as if it were midwinter. People scraped off bark for the livestock, but they were perishing by the dozens in their stalls. No one knew when it would end.[12]

But when Kristin succeeds in wearing Lavrans down so that he relents, her father brings her out to witness the rains, which have finally arrived to melt the snow and bring relief to the inhabitants of the valley:

> "Get up," he said quietly. "Do you hear it?"

> Then she heard the singing at the corners of the house—the deep, full tone of the moisture-laden south wind. Water was streaming off the roof, and the rain whispered as it fell on soft, melting snow.

> Kristin threw on a dress and followed her father to the outer door. Together they stood and looked out into the bright May night. Warm wind and rain swept toward them. The sky was a heap of tangled, surging rain clouds; there was a seething from

12. Undset, 238.

the woods, a whistling between the buildings. And upon the mountains they heard the hollow rumble of snow sliding down.

Kristin reached for her father's hand and held it. He had called her and wanted to show her this. It was the kind of thing he would have done in the past, before things changed between them. And now he was doing it again.[13]

It is amazing enough to see such intricacy and beauty in a Flannery O'Connor short story or a Gerard Manley Hopkins poem, where we can more readily appreciate how no word or detail is lost. But to discern such elaborate structural and aesthetic architecture in a novel of over a thousand pages is positively a marvel, and it makes reading *Kristin Lavransdatter* an unparalleled experience.

The novel repeatedly places Kristin's stubborn self-will in opposition to God's abundant mercy. Time and again, Kristin makes serious mistakes with far-reaching consequences, yet she refuses the path of mercy and instead is harsher on herself than God is. She is continually chastised by priests for her spiritual pride; as Gunnulf, the priestly brother of Erlend, rebukes her: "Are you so arrogant that you think yourself capable of sinning so badly that God's mercy is not great enough?"[14] She is quick to judge others, to find in their sin a ready excuse for her own failings. She is particularly harsh on her lover and later husband Erlend, who acts more like a relic of Norway's heathen Viking past than a medieval Christian landowner. She continually measures Erlend—as a husband, a father, an estate manager—against her own father, Lavrans, and as we come to expect, Erlend is always found wanting. Though we know his actions are gravely immoral, we are tempted to make concessions for Erlend, because we see the bad examples he has had, his poor formation, and his

13. Undset, 238–239.
14. Undset, 361.

confused attempts to meet Kristin's strict expectations. He feels suffocated by Kristin and her unforgiving nature. "If Erlend was in a mood to bear her irritability with good humor and gentleness, it would annoy her that he wasn't taking her words seriously. On some other day he might have little patience, and then his temper would flare, but she would respond with bitterness and coldness."[15] Quite simply, Erlend cannot win. Kristin, by contrast, has been given so much and should know better.

Indeed, I have had several women tell me that they put the novel down (or even threw it across the room!) in frustration with Kristin's melodrama. Kristin is, especially early on, a bit of a "drama queen"—but that is part of the point. She wants to compel God both to give her what she wants *and* to punish her severely for her sins when her self-will inevitably results in disaster for her and those whom she loves. The result is a soul in constant conflict with itself: "She would humble herself before God and Holy Olav with a burning fervor; she would hasten to do good, striving to force tears of true remorse from her eyes as she prayed. But each time she would feel that unthawed discontent in her heart."[16]

Because of its female protagonist and rich treatment of motherhood, some have suggested that *Kristin Lavransdatter* is best suited to a female reading audience, particularly mothers. It is true that there is arguably no other novel—modern, Catholic, or otherwise—that treats of the trials and triumphs of motherhood with such depth and sensitivity:

> They had been as healthy as little fledglings, all three of her
> sons—until the sickness had come to the region last summer.
> . . . For five days she had sat near the bed on the south wall where
> they lay, all three of them, with red spots covering their faces
> and with feverish eyes that shunned the light. Their small bodies
> were burning hot. She sat with her hand under the coverlet and

15. Undset, 527.
16. Undset, 843.

patted the soles of Bjorgulf's feet while she sang and sang until her poor voice was no more than a whisper.[17]

Yet the novel encompasses so much more than motherhood, and while Kristin and her cares remain the central focus, the male characters—the saintly Brother Edvin; Kristin's father, Lavrans; her paramour and later husband, Erlend; her intended, Simon; the struggling priest Gunnulf; even Kristin's own sons—are drawn with compelling psychological and spiritual precision. Consider this description of Erlend's heathen restlessness:

> Now he longed only to go away to that strife-torn place. He yearned madly and wildly for that remote promontory and for the thundering sea surrounding the forelands of the north, for the endless coastline and the enormous fjords which could conceal all manner of traps and deceptions, for the people whose language he understood only slightly, for their sorcery and inconstancy and cunning, for war and the sea, and for the singing of weapons, both his own and his men's.[18]

As author David Warren confesses, "I have never read a novel in which I could see men so clearly through a searching woman's eyes; in which . . . I felt so judged."[19] Another early critic, W. Gore Allen, agrees, going so far as to suggest that Undset's "outstanding power is the ability to think, speak, and reason as a man."[20] More recently, Tyler Blanski, writing for *The Catholic Gentleman*, considers the novel positively oozing with masculine virility and declares it with self-conscious hyperbole (the exact opposite of

17. Undset, 466.

18. Undset, 484.

19. David Warren, "Kristin Lavransdatter," Catholic Education Resource Center, March 21, 2019, https://www.catholiceducation.org/en/culture/literature /kristin-lavransdatter.html.

20. W. Gore Allen, *Renaissance in the North* (New York: Sheed and Ward, 1946), 51.

WOMEN OF THE CATHOLIC IMAGINATION

Viking male understatement and restraint) a must-read for all manly men: "A sweeping tale of fatherhood and farming, priests and sacraments and towering cathedrals, sacrifice and holy pilgrimages," he declares, "those men who have read this epic trilogy might as well have sprinkled fertilizer on their chests."[21] In the end, while the novel impresses with its rich portrayal of manliness and motherhood (and so much more), it is simply the flawed yet striving humanity of all the central characters—their sins, struggles, triumphs, and tragedies—that ultimately engages every reader.

A TALE OF TWO TRANSLATIONS

Since the first volume of Tiina Nunnally's updated translation, *The Wreath*, was published in 1997, the Penguin edition has been considered the authoritative version of *Kristin Lavransdatter*. The initial three volumes are now housed in a single, 1,146-page, hulking, rosemaling-covered tome (the audio version, narrated by Erin Bennett, runs to forty-five hours). Nunnally considered the original translation of Kristin by Charles Archer and J.S. Scott "severely flawed,"[22] both because she thought its archaic diction did not accurately reflect Undset's straightforward prose, and because several episodes, including some of the more "steamy" bits between Kristin and Erlend, were either toned down or expurgated. Her translation is now introducing new generations of readers to Undset's masterpiece. Indeed, journalist Rod Dreher declared the older translation "fusty" (apparently without ever having read it) and insists that readers acquire the Nunnally translation.[23]

21. Tyler Blanski, "Kristin Lavransdatter and Your Nordic Medieval Catholic Heart," *The Catholic Gentleman*, February 11, 2015, https://catholicgentleman .com/2015/02/kristin-lavransdatter-nordic-medieval-catholic-heart/.

22. Tiina Nunnally, "A Note on the Translation," in Undset, *Kristin Lavransdatter*, xx.

23. Rod Dreher, "Kristin Lavransdatter," Rod Dreher's Diary Substack, November 6, 2020, https://roddreher.substack.com/p/kristin-lavransdatter.

Yet assuming you choose the arguably more "accessible" Nunnally translation (which is the version quoted throughout this chapter), it is well worth seeking out and reading a used copy of the original translation. After all, it is the version that was published in Undset's lifetime, the version that so captivated converts like Dorothy Day and Deal Hudson. I first read *Kristin* in the Archer and Scott translation; the supposed "artificiality" of the medieval diction quickly fell away, in the same way that the mannered speech of Austen's characters does, and the power of the story overtook me. Archer's translation better preserves the "proverbial" texture of Norse speech so dominant in the saga tradition that inspired Undset and that provides much of the moral framework in the novel. In the earlier translation, for instance, when young Kristin overhears the conversation between her mother, Ragnfrid, and Fru Aashild, the latter reminds Ragnfrid not to dwell on her past missteps, for one cannot get pleasure in this brief life without some risk: "'No doing without some rueing, Ragnfrid,' said Lady Aashild."[24] This is rendered in the Nunnally translation as "'No bargain is without some loss, Ragnfrid,'"[25] flattening out the central notion of regret and repentance implied in a word like "rue," and sacrificing the rhyming nature that made this little bit of (flawed) advice stick with me as a young woman. A little later, when Ragnfrid confesses her sordid past to her saintly husband, Lavrans, she recalls an old ballad in which a man returns from hell, where he had heard a horrible groaning sound that turned out to be "the querns of untrue women grinding mould for their husband's meat." "All these years I have thought upon those words," said Ragnfrid. "Every day 'twas as though my heart was bleeding, for every day methought I ground you mould for meat."[26] In the newer translation, this is rendered as: "unfaithful

24. Sigrid Undset, *Kristin Lavransdatter*, vol. 1, *The Bridal Wreath*, trans. Charles Archer and J.S. Scott (New York: Alfred Knopf, 1923), 45.

25. Undset, *Kristin Lavransdatter*, trans. Nunnally, 50.

26. Undset, *Kristin Lavransdatter*, trans. Archer, 271.

wives ground up earth for their husband's food. . . . I felt as if I were grinding up earth for your food."[27] The use of the Norse-derived words "quern" (*kvern*) and "mould" (*mold*) and the alliteration in the Archer version seemed to me to make the passage even more immediate and powerful. As Undset herself says in *Return to the Future*, "We Norwegians were always given to proverbs; in proverbs the experiences of our tribes and the wisdom of our fathers were transmitted from generation to generation."[28] Some of that wisdom seems regrettably, if not intentionally, "squeezed out" of the Nunnally translation in order to make room for a modern "feel" to the novel. And when Nunnally sums up the book as simply a "magnificent story of a headstrong young woman who defies her family and faith to follow the passions of her heart,"[29] it is hard not to suspect that the translator is rather deaf to the novel's central message, with implications for the translation's sensitivity to Undset's rich portrayal of faith.[30] Many devoted readers thus still retain a fondness for the "fusty" version, as I do.

"A REMEDY FOR OUR MISERY"

After the outbreak of the Second World War, Undset fled Norway and spent five years in the United States, living in a Brooklyn apartment and furthering her work as an apologist for both the Catholic Church and the Allies. Her fiction-writing career had come abruptly to a close. When she returned to Norway in 1945, her health and spirit had been buffeted by suffering: her son, Anders, had been killed near her home shortly after the Nazi invasion; her beloved estate of Bjerkebaek had been used as a brothel by the Nazis, the desk her father had built her burnt for firewood.

27. Undset, *Kristin Lavransdatter*, trans. Nunnally, 291.

28. Sigrid Undset, *Return to the Future*, trans. Henriette C.K. Naeseth (New York: Alfred Knopf, 1942), 210.

29. Tiina Nunnally, "A Note on the Translation," xx.

30. The "List of Holy Days" at the close of the novel, for instance, still incorrectly lists St. Stefan's Day as December 25 rather than December 26.

Undset had every reason to be bitter and resentful toward God, to cut herself off from human and divine companionship. Yet she managed somehow to persevere. As she wrote to friend and fellow novelist Willa Cather shortly after her return to Norway, "Your picture which Alfred Knopf sent me from you years ago I also unearthed from the attic, where my 'roomers' had put away pele-mele the things they did not want—which was not much. It is a little broken and soiled, but all the more dear to me."[31]

Undset's final literary labor of love was a biography of St. Catherine of Siena. The manuscript was rejected by Doubleday in her lifetime but was published posthumously in Norwegian in 1951 and then in English in 1954 by Sheed and Ward. When Undset herself became a Dominican tertiary in 1928, she took the name Olave, the feminine of her beloved St. Olav. The life of St. Catherine, that great female medieval Dominican saint and Doctor of the Church, had always captivated Undset, and in her account of the saint's early life we can discern obvious similarities to the fictional Kristin. Catherine is a "grown girl now, on the threshold of womanhood"; the devil comes to her "in the likeness of a young man, not to frighten her but to persuade." He shows her all the finery the Italian craftsmen have to offer her: "Catherine stared at these examples of earthly magnificence—symbols of the power and the joy the world can offer a young woman who is attractive and intelligent, with boundless possibilities of experiencing passion and love."[32] Instead of accepting the world, Catherine "threw herself before the crucifix and begged her Bridegroom to come to her help." Our Lady then appears to Catherine, offering her a heavenly cloak; a few days later, "Catherine Benincasa received the white robe and veil which stand for purity of body and soul, and the black cape which is the symbol of humility and death to

31. Sigrid Undset, Letter of March 17, 1946, quoted in Sherill Harbison, "Sigrid Undset and Willa Cather: A Friendship," *Willa Cather Pioneer Memorial Newsletter and Review* 42, no. 3 (Winter–Spring 1999): 54.

32. Sigrid Undset, *Catherine of Siena*, trans. Kate Austin-Lund (San Francisco: Ignatius, 2009), 36.

this world."[33] When faced with a similar temptation, the beautiful young Kristin makes a different choice: "She loved the world and longed for the world. . . . She was unwilling to give up her inheritance of health and beauty and love."[34] The thousand pages of Undset's novel chronicle, with raw and compelling artistry, the dramatic tension between Kristin's unwillingness and her sincere striving for holiness.

In Undset's life and writings, then, the scandal of the cross becomes the only cure for the scandal of self-love. "For us," Undset tells us, "Catherine would have only the same message which she brought to her contemporaries, she would know only of the same remedy for our misery—the blood of Christ, the fire of God's love, which burns up self-love and self-will, and lets the soul appear, beautiful and full of grace, as it was meant to be when God created us."[35] For most of us, though, subduing the fires of self-love is not the work of an instant, as it was for St. Catherine of Siena, but of a lifetime, as it is for Undset's fictional Kristin. We stumble; we start again. Like most of us, Kristin commits some astonishingly selfish and sinful acts throughout her life; like most of us, her moments of spiritual clarity and self-knowledge are hard-won and brief. But God's mercy is boundless and unfathomable, and Kristin's journey to God is forged in the fires of suffering, slowly purified over the course of a lifetime:

> It seemed to her a mystery that she could not comprehend, but she was certain that God had held her firmly in a pact which had been made for her, without her knowing it, from a love that had been poured over her—and in spite of her willfulness, in spite of her melancholy, earthbound heart, some of that love had stayed inside her, had worked on her like sun on the earth,

33. Undset, 37.
34. Undset, *Kristin Lavransdatter*, trans. Nunnally, 68.
35. Undset, 85.

had driven forth a crop that neither the fiercest fire of passion nor its stormiest anger could completely destroy.[36]

RECOMMENDED READING

Sigrid Undset. *Catherine of Siena.*

_____. *Gunnar's Daughter.*

_____. *Kristin Lavransdatter.*

_____. *The Master of Hestviken.*

Amy Fahey teaches literature at the Thomas More College of Liberal Arts in Merrimack, New Hampshire. She holds a BA in English Literature and Christian Studies from Hillsdale College, an MPhil in Mediaeval Literature from the University of St. Andrews, and an MA and PhD in English and American Literature from Washington University in St. Louis. Dr. Fahey has written and lectured on Joyce Kilmer, G.K. Chesterton, Sigrid Undset, Flannery O'Connor, and other Catholic writers. Her work has appeared in *The Catholic Herald, The St. Austin Review, The Catholic Thing, Crisis Magazine, Columbia Magazine,* and elsewhere.

---

36. Undset, 1122.

Caryll Houselander:
Divine Eccentric

Julia Meszaros

Caryll Houselander (1901–1954) was a mystic, artist, writer, and spiritual counselor. She made wooden statues, crucifixes, and cribs, and she drew, painted, and illustrated books. Her spiritual writings were so successful that, for many years, she was Sheed and Ward's best-selling author. Houselander wrote her first novel only later in life, and her early death cut short her career as a writer of fiction. Yet, together with her many short stories, her novel, *The Dry Wood*, forms an important contribution to the Catholic literary movement. Despite their intense popularity during the 1940s and '50s, Houselander's writings eventually fell out of print—in part, perhaps, on account of their emphasis on the meaning of spiritual and physical suffering, which did not suit the postconciliar spirit, yet which is as relevant today as ever. More recently, her writings have been rediscovered and are now mostly back in print.

CARYLL HOUSELANDER: "THAT DIVINE ECCENTRIC"

Born to agnostic parents, Houselander came into the Catholic Church at nine years old, when her mother converted through the influence of the Catholic family doctor, Dr. Paley, and a close family friend, Smoky. Although an agnostic, Smoky was convinced that "if Jesus Christ was really God, and if he founded a Church" this had to be the Roman Catholic Church.[1] Mrs. Houselander and her two daughters entered the Church largely uninstructed in the faith, which they practiced through an eclectic array of devotions, rituals, and charitable works. Shortly after her "rather odd reception into the Church," the young Caryll underwent the great trauma of her parents' divorce.[2] From thereon, she was sent to various convent schools, interspersed with many sick leaves, and finally, at age sixteen, was called home to help her mother care for a troubled priest. Happening in quick succession, these two formative childhood events—Houselander's reception into the Church and the loss of her family home—marked the beginning of a life of neurosis, aggravated by constant physical illness and pain. Her parents' divorce shattered her childlike trust in God; and yet her reception of the sacraments ignited an intense desire to know and find Christ.

During the First World War, while attending a French convent school, Houselander had what can be described as a mystical vision: she saw a Bavarian nun, whom the war had made an outcast in the French convent, bowed under a crown of thorns and undergoing "inconsolable grief."[3] A couple of years later, running an errand in the summer of 1918, Caryll was suddenly stopped in her tracks and, though never before having seen a Russian icon, saw a "gigantic and living [. . .] icon of Christ the King crucified" spread over her colorless London street; Christ's "beautiful face stood sharp with grief . . . but the eyes and the mouth smiled with the ineffable love which consumes sorrow and

1. Caryll Houselander, *A Rocking Horse Catholic* (New York: Sheed and Ward, 1955), 19.
2. Houselander, 16.
3. Houselander, 55–56.

pain."[4] The following day, she learned that the Russian emperor and his family were killed the night before. More surprisingly, she discovered that the face of the murdered tsar was identical with that of Christ in her vision.

Although Caryll's visions left her convinced that Christ's life, including his Passion, continues in human lives today, Houselander's faith was at this time deeply shaken by the unchristian behavior she received at the hands of 'good Catholics' who (falsely) saw scandal in her mother's decision to take in the 'derelict' priest and who condemned and socially ostracized the entire household as a result.[5] Houselander never doubted Christ's Real Presence in the Eucharist but nonetheless began to look for Christ outside of the Catholic Church while attending art school and supporting herself. She explored all forms of Christianity as well as Buddhism and Judaism and developed a particular love for the Russian Church. Yet, whatever beauty was present in those faiths, she reluctantly found herself in agreement with her friend Smoky that Catholicism is "the only religion in the world that includes all that is beautiful and good in every other, and all the poetry that is innate in the human race."[6]

During this time of religious seeking, however, Houselander had starved herself of the sacraments and felt at home among her fellow Bohemian artists, many of whom she found more Christlike than her Catholic acquaintances. When caught up in the one romantic entanglement of her life—with the famous British spy Sidney Reilly—she was tempted to fully remove herself from the Church. Three events conspired to prevent this. Reilly abruptly married another woman, and Caryll was once more confronted with questions of love, loneliness, and suffering. Also, during one of her long strolls through London, she encountered Frank Sheed speaking for the Catholic Evidence Guild at Hyde Park corner and

4. Houselander, 86–87.
5. Houselander, 78–80.
6. Houselander, 20.

instinctively saw that here she found an authentic Catholicism: "the Church being Christ . . . Christ following his lost sheep."[7]

And finally, around this time, Caryll had her last, and most powerful, vision. On a London underground train packed with exhausted workers she suddenly saw "with [her] mind, but as vividly as a wonderful picture, Christ in them all. . . . Not only was Christ in every one of them, living in them, dying in them, rejoicing in them, sorrowing in them—but because He was in them, and because they were here, the whole world was here too, here in this underground train."[8] Caryll at once understood the presence of Christ in absolutely everyone: "Christ in His perfect human nature, Christ in his risen glory *and* Christ in His need and His suffering on earth."[9] This realization allowed her to see that Christ is present even in "those sinners whose souls seem to be dead"—namely the dead "Christ in the tomb," who is "potentially the risen Christ."[10]

Fully reunited with the Catholic Church, Houselander developed a great compassion for all who suffer: sinners, orphans, neurotics, the poor. Reinforced by her immensely popular writings, this meant she was at times almost besieged by people seeking her company and conversation and maintained a vast correspondence as well as a varied circle of friends from all sorts of backgrounds—privileged members of the upper class, Bohemian artists, Catholics, ordinary workers. Priests and doctors sought her help for psychologically distressed persons and traumatized orphans for whom they could do no more. Despite craving solitude and quiet for her art, Houselander attended to them all, at times being able to write only at night in the tiny bathroom of her crowded one-room apartment. As the distinguished psychologist and neurologist Dr. Eric Strauss put it, she "loved them back

7. Houselander, 102.
8. Houselander, 105–106.
9. Houselander, 106.
10. Houselander, 106.

into life" by suffering with them and giving them "not only love but the full realization that love had gone out to them and was surrounding them."[11]

Friends said of her that, especially during and after the war, Houselander truly "offered herself up to be burnt."[12] She had few possessions and barely ate or slept, instead giving away her rations, volunteering to fire-watch after long days at her first aid post, and endlessly giving her time to those in need. She never missed daily Mass and weekly confession and, although generally skeptical of religious movements, founded one such movement, called the *Sprats*. It was their mission to help those whom the war had pushed to the brink of existence without hurting their pride in doing so. With a group of helpers that grew to several hundred, she devised the most complicated schemes to covertly bring aid to people in need.

Houselander's life was as intensely intellectual as it was practical and spiritual. From early on, she saw these dimensions as linked: "Learn, as the Catechism says, to know [God], then the rest will follow," she wrote in one of her dialogues. "If you *do* know God as He is, you can't help loving Him and serving Him—and it is so for others, for the blind, hungry, desperate, human race, looking to us for the knowledge of God."[13]

Houselander remained a single laywoman throughout her life. Yet she led the ascetic and rigorously disciplined life of a nun and brought countless people into the Church. At the same time, Houselander remained a sharp-tongued bohemian. She drank, smoked, and was notorious for her odd appearance: bright red

11. Maisie Ward, *Caryll Houselander: That Divine Eccentric* (New York: Sheed and Ward, 1962), 10, 188.

12. Ward, 11.

13. Caryll Houselander, quoted in Ward, 117. She also acknowledged the role knowing doctrine played in her returning to and keeping the faith despite her ill feelings toward some of her fellow Catholics: "For me it had always been of absolute necessity to have an *instructed* mind: without that, religion could not be a thing of the will, which it must be if it is to endure" (Houselander, *A Rocking Horse Catholic*, 74).

bangs, round spectacles, and pure white face-powder: a "divine eccentric." It is no overstatement to say that her life offers a unique model of sanctity for lay men and women, especially artists.

BRINGING THE BODY OF CHRIST ALIVE IN FICTION

Houselander wrote in the hope of helping souls. Her body of writing spans numerous books of spiritual writings, poetry, meditations on the Rosary and the Stations of the Cross, as well as articles and stories for magazines, such as the *Messenger of the Sacred Heart*, the *Children's Messenger*, and *Grail Magazine*, and one novel. All of it is centered around Christ's presence in human beings. Christ's life continues in human lives today, Houselander insists: his infancy in the helpless and innocent, his passion in the poor and afflicted, his death in those alienated from God, his Resurrection in those who renew the world.

This theme first comes to real prominence in *This War Is the Passion* (1941). Written and published during the Second World War, Houselander argues that the suffering endured on account of the war is nothing less than "[Christ's] Passion going on now."[14] This means that it is not wasted and that, insofar as it cannot be alleviated, it should be accepted. Resenting it would be like Peter looking to deter Christ from the Passion and thereby undermining God's plan of redemption.[15] Houselander can successfully make such a bold argument because she herself is in terror during every London raid, because she writes as someone who knows the hardship of poverty, loneliness, and neurosis, and because she seeks to relieve the suffering of others as much as she tries to accept her own. As Maisie Ward writes, this became "Caryll's favourite meditation—we fallen men and women brought suffering into the world, caused suffering to Christ. But

14. Caryll Houselander, *The Letters of Caryll Houselander*, ed. Maisie Ward (New York: Sheed and Ward, 1965), 4.

15. Caryll Houselander, *The Reed of God* (New York: Sheed and Ward, 1944), 77.

now our suffering can itself become redemptive because Christ suffers *in* us—the members of His Mystical Body."[16]

It was obvious to Houselander that it is difficult to suffer willingly. It becomes possible when what she calls the "seed" of Christ is allowed to take root and flower in the human soul.[17] A meditation on the life of Our Lady, her book *The Reed of God* (1944) offers an account of *how* to live life in this Christian way. By giving human life to the Son of God, Mary gave him hands and feet, a body to suffer. We must do the same, Houselander argues. We must become virginal or empty, like Mary, so as to truly receive Christ into ourselves and then, in an Advent season of quiet, let the Christ-seed take root and grow in us until we have truly given him *our* hands and feet, *our* body to suffer in, so that he may save the world. If we lose Christ again, we must, like Our Lady, go out and look for him—until we have become one with him once more.

This focus on letting Christ live in every part of our lives is further developed in *The Comforting of Christ* (1946) and *The Passion of the Infant Christ* (1949). One of its implications is that all human activities, including work, should be open to receiving Christ and then bringing him back into the world:

> The great tragedy that has resulted from modern methods of industry is that the creativeness of Advent has been left out of work. Production no longer means a man making something that he has conceived in his own heart. . . . No man should ever make anything except in the spirit in which a woman bears a child, in the spirit in which Christ was formed in Mary's womb, in the love with which God created the world. The integral goodness and fittingness of the work of a man's hands or mind is sacred.[18]

16. Ward, *That Divine Eccentric*, 225.

17. Houselander, *The Reed of God*, 62, 71.

18. Houselander, 35.

Houselander considers this to be especially true of art, the artist being perhaps the last person left to witness to the beauty of doing something for its own sake, no matter the cost.

Houselander sees that even once the war and its more visceral challenges are over, this spiritual task of bringing Christ into the world is no easier. On the contrary, it becomes obvious that people are suffering from ailments even more debilitating than physical suffering: anxiety, neurosis, guilt. In her book *Guilt* (1951), Houselander reads mental illness as a disease of the soul caused by our materialistic age. For too long, people "have ceased to exercise the spiritual part of their nature. . . . They have not allowed their souls to function at all," thereby causing them to become sick.[19] Men and women today no longer know *who* and *why* they are; they do not know themselves as made in God's image and, since Freud, they struggle to understand that their feelings of guilt are rooted in a reality—in human sinfulness.[20] And yet, the mentally sick "may be far closer to God than the mentally healthy" because, like with physical sickness, the sufferer can "offer his illness itself as both prayer and heavy penance."[21] Houselander appears to attribute all mental illness to spiritual (as opposed to biological) causes—to misdirected feelings of the same guilt shared, in fact, by all sinners. For the mentally ill, as for the regular sinner, healing is only to be found in the context of the knowledge that we are made for union with Christ: "Realization of our oneness in Christ is the only cure for human loneliness."[22] Only this allows us "to give one another our voices, to carry one another in our arms, to take one another's place before God, to give Christ to one another and to be Christ for one another."[23]

19. Caryll Houselander, *Guilt* (New York: Sheed and Ward, 1951), xi.

20. Houselander, 147.

21. Ward, *That Divine Eccentric*, 273.

22. Houselander, *A Rocking Horse Catholic*, 107.

23. Houselander, *Guilt*, 199.

HOUSELANDER'S FICTION: HER SHORT STORIES AND HER NOVEL

Houselander's stories were written for magazines and later collected and published posthumously as *Inside the Ark* (1956), *Terrible Farmer Timson* (1957), and *Bird on the Wing* (1958). Then and now these tended to be thought of as children's stories (partly, surely, because they all involve children). But in fact they are so profound in content and mysterious in style that adults will be anything but bored by them. They offer various imaginative narratives explaining why "unless you change and become like children, you will never enter the kingdom of heaven" (Matt. 18:3).

In "Terrible Farmer Timson," for instance, two children have the courage farmer Timson lacks and offer it up for him. They are able to do so on account of their faith and love of Christ. In this way, two members of Christ's Mystical Body supplement what another lacks and thereby reunite him with Christ. But Houselander's stories also meditate on the fact that it is not only the members of Christ's Body who make up for one another's shortcomings but Christ himself who does the same: when, in "The Curé's Guest," Jean and Marie Angèle mock the village priest and refuse Christ, the Christ-child mystically appears to the priest as the joyful, loving children God made them to be. This is possible because of the priest's own will to see Christ in them. Thus, in one way or another, genuine desire for communion with Christ will always be answered.[24] And yet, in all these stories, Christ wants to come into the world through the ordinary human beings who make up his Body. Their ordinary circumstances, such as their poverty, prove to be more of an aid than a hindrance to their ability to mediate Christ. "If I Were You," for instance, tells of why human beings are less receptive to a Savior arriving in kingly splendor than to a simple boy.

24. Caryll Houselander, *Catholic Tales for Boys and Girls* (Manchester, NH: Sophia Institute, 2002).

Even while writing these stories, Houselander's focus lay on her spiritual and psychological writings. After the war, however, this emphasis shifted. She no longer wanted to "preach" to her fellows: "I prefer writing fiction: it's more like a big gesture of sympathy —like taking hold of another sinner's hand and pressing it lovingly as we walk together."[25] It is at this point that Houselander wrote her first novel, *The Dry Wood* (1947). Although *The Dry Wood* occasionally still manifests the homiletic or didactic tone more proper to spiritual writings, it is a timeless and unforgettable novel that deserves a prominent place not only in the canons of Catholic writing but in Anglo-American modernist literature. It approaches greatness in its structure and design and in the brilliance of its author's powers of description—of place, event, atmosphere. Meditating on the presence of Christ in every human being and on how that presence is brought alive, it illustrates her generosity of spirit and offers a message at once realist and hopeful.

The Dry Wood is set in Riverside, an impoverished East London docklands parish around the 1940s. The parish's saintly priest, Fr. Malone, has recently died, and one of its most-loved members, seven-year-old Willie Jewel, is dying too. The novel spans a nine-day novena the parish prays to Fr. Malone for Willie's life and takes the reader into the lives of various members of the community and their struggles, all of whom stand in some relationship with Willie: his parents, his doctor, the parish priest, various parishioners who have cared for him over the years, a new convert, a merchant, as well as Willie's bishop and a monsignor, who have conflicting ideas about the novena.

CHRIST IN ALL: SUFFERING, LOVE, AND REDEMPTION

Willie Jewel is clearly a Christ-figure, and his parents modern images of Mary and Joseph. Through Willie, Houselander

25. Houselander, in Ward, *That Divine Eccentric*, 223.

masterfully evokes at one and the same time the infant Christ in his helpless love and the crucified Christ in his innocent suffering. He is a "living crucifix" and, in a sense, the heart of the Riverside parish. But the novel's other characters, too, represent Christ at various stages of his life. Fr. Malone is the risen Christ, and his successor, Fr. O'Grady, is Christ wandering the earth, ministering to his flock; Timothy, a young convert, is the newly baptized Christ, and Rose O'Shane, a drunk, is the humiliated Christ; Carmel Fernandez can be read as Christ having fallen under the weight of his cross, and the self-righteous monsignor and the rationalist Dr. Moncrieff are Christ dead in the tomb, with the potential to rise again.

Equally central is the novel's daring exploration of the meaning of human suffering, indeed, of its redemptive power. With great sensitivity and reverence, *The Dry Wood* convincingly suggests that this is especially true of the suffering of an innocent child: "In Willie Jewel Caryll depicted a child *accepting*, whose death becomes one with Christ's and wins joy, peace and triumph for others."[26] The character of Willie allows the reader to see that through such loving acceptance of innocent suffering a person becomes so like Christ—that Christ is so alive in that person (see Gal. 2:20)—that he or she becomes the community's "hope of glory" (Col. 1:27), a Christ-bearer who participates in Christ's redemptive work.

Although this is one of Christianity's most central claims, it is very difficult to reflect on conceptually. Theologians traditionally speak of an economy of salvation. This refers to the Catholic belief that our prayers, sacrifices, or acts of charity, when united with Christ and moved by the Holy Spirit, help atone for our and others' sins and merit certain goods or graces. Since this can be abused for encouraging innocent suffering or condoning terrible injustice, theologians after the two world wars tended to downplay or avoid

26. Ward, 225.

this doctrinal terrain. This makes Houselander's imaginative treatment of this difficult subject through the means of fiction all the more valuable. For instead of arguing a point, *The Dry Wood* beautifully and persuasively shows that, when coupled with the joy and love of Christ, weakness, helplessness, and affliction can contribute to our redemption from the bonds of sin.

In *Guilt*, she later wrote:

> The real cause of frustration, of the lack of fulfilment and the failure of human beings as human beings, is the will not to suffer. In proportion to our willingness to suffer we succeed as human beings; we fail in proportion to our will not to suffer. This, because it is the will to accept suffering which liberates the capacity to love, and on the capacity to love, and on that alone, our fulfilment as human beings depends.[27]

The Dry Wood illustrates how love and the will to suffer are mutually reinforcing. It is his natural love for his son that enables Willie's father to prevail in his labors, and, likewise, it is his love for Christ that drives Fr. O'Grady's acts of self-denial. Yet the various characters' willingness to suffer in turn inspires an even greater, almost heroic love. This is most profoundly the case in Willie's suffering, which is entirely innocent and whose fruits are thus most purely for others: joined with Christ's, his suffering completes "what is lacking in Christ's afflictions for the sake of his body, that is, the church" (Col. 1:24). Suffering, *The Dry Wood* makes clear, is not God's will. But, as Fr. O'Grady says in his final sermon, "God in His Mercy uses these things for love." The saint "does not *choose* suffering at all, but he accepts it without conditions, because he surrenders himself to life and his personal destiny and makes no conditions."[28]

27. Houselander, *Guilt*, 124.
28. Houselander, 131.

THE MYSTICAL BODY IN THE MODERN WORLD

In order to show how human beings are united in Christ's Mystical Body despite their worldly disconnectedness, *The Dry Wood* skillfully uses modernist literary innovations regarding structure and voice in a highly original manner. Each chapter focuses on a different member of the community. This creates a sense of disjointedness; the community is disparate or fractured, and each member experiences isolation or even loneliness. However, not only does the narrative voice lay over this a Catholic sense of the uniqueness and dignity of each individual, but by interweaving each character's personal suffering with the community's prayers for Willie, Houselander also shows how their lives are gathered up and united in Christ even if they do not always experience this. By the time of the novel's final Mass, it is clear that, while every individual's hardship is real, it is also embedded in the bigger reality of a communion of which glimpses are caught wherever we rally around Christ. Houselander in this way utilizes modernist techniques to create the reality of the Catholic life of faith as something that occurs at different levels of reality simultaneously: the solitary and collective, the earthly and divine, the pedestrian and liturgical.

Houselander's use of modernist technique for Catholic ends is indicative of her relationship with modernity in general. Where other Catholic writers are often simply dismissive of modernity, her faith compels her to tread more carefully. She felt that "the modernist writers are not the contemptible egoists which they are too often supposed to be" but rather suffer from the materialism that besets our entire age.[29] The struggles of the modern age are shared, and felt all the more acutely, also by Catholics, for they stem from a dehumanizing idolization of "the machine" and an ignorance of God.[30] Houselander finds herself "tortured": she

29. Houselander, in Ward, *That Divine Eccentric*, 108.
30. Houselander, in Ward, 115.

refuses to "range [her]self among those who, though they clearly share my desires, do not share my faith in Christ," yet feels equally certain that she must nonetheless keep looking for Christ in today's world.[31]

CONCLUSION

Houselander's one novel poetically draws together the entire range of themes present in her spiritual writings. In addition to the above, it illustrates the Marian nature of every Christian life and also the way in which every Christian is a child before God. It engages with the particular vocation of the priest alongside the priesthood of all believers. It manifests Houselander's skepticism of religious movements and her equal disagreement with, and compassion for, those who reject Christ. It spells out the effects of ego-neurosis and scientific rationalism, and it highlights Houselander's particular love for the natural world, frequently using botanical images to speak about the life of the spirit.

Above all, *The Dry Wood* portrays holiness not as a sanitized ideal but as an unassuming reality that emerges from allowing Christ into the regular failures, joys, and hardships of ordinary life. Given that the novel form is typically more suited to showing human depravity than holiness, this is no small feat. *The Dry Wood* is both modern and Catholic, both experimental and traditional. Reading it is a lesson in hope, for it allows the reader to see Christ at work in human lives even where neither outward circumstances nor inner experience suggest this. And it is a lesson in charity, because it invites the reader to recognize Christ in all human beings, even those most difficult to tolerate. It can do so because its mystical author saw

---

31. Houselander, in Ward, 109.

Earth crammed with heaven
And every common bush afire with God.[32]

RECOMMENDED READING

Fiction

Caryll Houselander. *Bird on the Wing.*
_____. *The Dry Wood.*
_____. *Inside the Ark.*
_____. *Terrible Farmer Timson and Other Stories.* (Republished in 2002 as *Catholic Tales for Boys and Girls* by Sophia Institute Press.)

Spiritual Writings

Caryll Houselander. *The Comforting of Christ.*
_____. *Guilt.*
_____. *The Passion of the Infant Christ.*
_____. *The Reed of God.*
_____. *The Risen Christ.*
_____. *This War Is the Passion.*

Poetry

Caryll Houselander. *The Flowering Tree.*

Autobiography

Caryll Houselander. *A Rocking Horse Catholic.*

Other

Maisie Ward. *Caryll Houselander: That Divine Eccentric.*
_____, ed. *The Letters of Caryll Houselander.*

32. Houselander, in Ward, 146.

Julia Meszaros teaches systematic theology at St Patrick's Pontifical University, Maynooth. With Bonnie Lander Johnson she edits *Catholic Women Writers*, a Catholic University of America Press multivolume series that puts the women of the Catholic Literary Revival back into print and has published writings by some of the women represented in this volume. Meszaros has written numerous articles in the fields of theological anthropology and theology and literature and is the author of *Selfless Love and Human Flourishing in Paul Tillich and Iris Murdoch* (Oxford University Press, 2016).

Gertrud von le Fort:
Undaunted Ambassador
of Grace

Helena M. Tomko

Gertrud von le Fort's memoir tells only half her story. The German novelist and poet chose the title, *Half of Life* (1965), to warn her readers of this deliberate reticence. The memoir reveals only so much about her happy, aristocratic childhood in the late nineteenth century; her studies and friendships with important German intellectuals in the early years of the new century; and the trauma and grief she experienced following World War I. She stops short of describing her conversion to Catholicism in the mid-1920s, disappointing curious readers who knew her best as a prominent mid-century Catholic writer.

Her memoir's title also alludes to the melancholic poem of the same name by Friedrich Hölderlin (1770–1843), which laments a life at its midpoint. What will happen to everything we cultivate when autumnal abundance confronts the cold chill of winter—and the death it signifies? What will befall us in that other, declining half of life?

Alas, for where in winter
Shall I come by flowers and where
The sunlight
And shade of the earth?[1]

The poem's melancholy suits the mood of a forty-four-year-old le Fort in 1920. But she wrote her memoir forty-five years later, assured that the second half of her life had been an abundant response to any fear of wintery days to come. Beyond that biographical midpoint, le Fort had found sustenance in sacramental faith and an ecclesial life that would embolden her imagination. And she had discovered a creative freedom that transformed writing into her vocation.

In the final pages of the memoir, she bids farewell to her family's northern country estate, which was seized by the Mecklenburg authorities following her brother's foolhardy attempt to overthrow the new democratic government in the 1920 Kapp Putsch. Le Fort recalls the autumnal sight of wild swans beating their wings across the lake and feeling "the endless melancholy of uninterpretable events." She concedes, however, that this dark moment would bear fruit in her best-loved novella, *The Song at the Scaffold* (1931), a story that probes the theological depths of "abyssal world anxiety."[2] Addressing the Church as mystical person, le Fort would soon write in her *Hymns to the Church* (1924):

You bid me quench my only light and bid me rekindle it at the darkness of night—
You order me blindness that I may see and deafness that I may hear!
Do you know what you do?[3]

1. Friedrich Hölderlin, "Half of Life," in *Selected Poetry*, trans. David Constantine (Hexham, UK: Bloodaxe, 2018), 80.

2. Gertrud von le Fort, *Hälfte des Lebens* (Munich: Ehrenwirth, 1965), 148–151. Translations are mine, unless otherwise noted.

3. Gertrud von Le [sic] Fort, *Hymns to the Church*, trans. Margaret Chanler (New York: Sheed and Ward, 1942), 15.

Nothing in le Fort's writing makes sense without this *via negativa* through historical, national, and personal crisis, through suffering, abandonment, and anxiety, toward total surrender to Christ in the fullness of faith—and lifelong trust in the mysterious fruitfulness of this surrender.

CONVERSION

A late bloomer in her literary career, le Fort never lost her stylistic allegiance to the nineteenth century, even as she experimented with the trends of the twentieth. Born into an aristocratic family in 1876, Baroness von le Fort had grown up in a Prussian, imperial, and militaristic world. Her religious formation was defined by her mother's Lutheran devotion and delight in the hymnic verse of German Pietism. Le Fort's early writing was more pastime than profession, even after she began publishing in the years before World War I.

But by the time le Fort died on the Feast of All Souls in 1971, she had been a Catholic for half a century and a well-known writer for longer. She had lived through two world wars, shuddered at the rise of National Socialism, lived through its evils, and witnessed its collapse. The unified Germany of her birth had been divided between democracy in the West and communism in the East. The Second Vatican Council had been called and concluded. She had lost the privileges of her aristocratic birth but was now an award-winning national treasure. Her books had formed a generation—including the future Pope Benedict XVI, who affectionately recalled her influence during his seminary studies.[4] As Germany's precipitous secularization gained momentum, le Fort's popularity declined. Readers who once cherished her writing came to regard it with befuddlement, even disdain.

---

4. Joseph Ratzinger, *Milestones: Memoirs, 1927–77* (San Francisco: Ignatius, 1998), 42.

Le Fort's reception into the Catholic Church in March 1926 belongs to the inter-war period that saw many prominent conversions among German intellectuals. These converts include Edith Stein, who became le Fort's friend prior to Stein's entry into Carmelite religious life. While Stein arrived at Christian faith via her Jewish childhood, subsequent atheism, and philosophical inquiry, le Fort never lost the fervor of childhood piety. She inched toward Catholicism through study of Church history, her encounters with Benedictine liturgy, and the vigorous Munich-based Catholic culture she discovered in the early years of the Weimar Republic. Forever loyal to her "best friend," the liberal Protestant theologian Ernst Troeltsch, le Fort was also close to Friedrich Gogarten. Together with Karl Barth, Gogarten founded the Protestant movement known as dialectical theology, which rejected everything his teacher Troeltsch represented.[5] It was le Fort who inadvertently gave Gogarten the name for the movement's journal, *Between the Ages*, when she wrote to him in 1920 that she felt "not just outwardly but deeply inwardly a child of two ages and of two worlds."[6] Le Fort's sense of historical displacement also captures well the "in-betweenness" of her imagination, which often seems to have a surer grasp on things past than present, supernatural than natural. As the English Catholic publisher Frank Sheed would write, in her fiction "time is real but subordinated to, and occasionally altogether eclipsed by, eternity."[7]

Despite her proximity to these important Protestant figures, le Fort was drawing closer to Catholicism. In summer 1921, she told Gogarten how much she liked Romano Guardini's *On the Spirit of the Liturgy* (1918), a defining text for the twentieth-century

---

5. Le Fort, *Hälfte des Lebens*, 87, 92.

6. Gertrud von le Fort to Friedrich Gogarten, in *Gertrud von le Fort—Friedrich Gogarten: Briefwechsel, 1911–27*, ed. Horst Renz (Berlin: De Gruyter, 2022), 90, 125.

7. Frank Sheed, *Sidelights on the Catholic Revival* (London: Catholic Book Club, 1941), 117.

Catholic liturgical movement. She mused, rhetorically, "Are we really drawing nearer to the old Church?" Recovering from a nervous collapse caused by grief and trauma, she suggested to Gogarten that the sure theological footing they both sought would not be found within German Protestantism: "But where can it happen? . . . I feel more and more that everything that your fight concerns is much more at home in the Catholic Church, which has come close to me here in a significant way—and perhaps also because of my sickness."[8] Having settled in Baierbrunn, Bavaria, she found solace in the Liturgy of the Hours at the neighboring Benedictine monastery, where she befriended the monks. No doctrinal questions obstructed her full assent to Church teaching by this time. But it was the "sublimity of the liturgy and irrefutability of the ultimate grounds of faith" that would prove decisive for her eventual assent.[9]

The first literary fruits of le Fort's conversion are her *Hymns to the Church*, written between 1922 and 1924 as a "kind of lyric journal." A desperate soul dialogues with God, who responds in the voice of the Church. Le Fort explains that "the soul, who is still caught deep within herself, first hears this voice in her own meditations as an astonishing, shocking inner realization of the supernatural truth and love of the Church that bursts through her limitations."[10] The soul enters deeper into the sacred mysteries that have freed her. Le Fort's vision of the Church as interlocutor—as person—draws on what St. Paul calls the "great mystery" (Eph. 5:32) of the Church as, at once, Christ's Body and his Bride. This interlocutor is bridal and maternal, majestic and sacrificial:

8. Gogarten and le Fort, *Briefwechsel*, 112, 119.

9. Quoted in Helena M. Tomko, *Sacramental Realism: Gertrud von le Fort and German Catholic Literature in the Weimar Republic and Third Reich* (Leeds: Maney, 2007), 21.

10. Quoted in Helena M. Tomko, "The 'Golden-Hearted' Imagination of Gertrud von le Fort," *Logos* 23.2 (2020): 129–144, at 135.

But you return from the desert adorned as a bride, bathed in
    brightness from the wings of the night.
You come from the abyss as one living, from the eternal
    solitude as one whose prayers have been answered.
You return from destruction as one who has found strength,
    out of the invisible you return with form and stature.[11]

These paradoxes—beauty from the desert, brightness from darkness, life from the abyss, communion in solitude, strength from destruction, visibility from invisibility—explain why le Fort regarded her Psalm-like poems as the "true foundation" of her subsequent writing. Never bashful about the churchiness of her imagination, she invites readers to see how the mystical and prophetic can inform an ecclesiological understanding of the human person, real or fictional.

Conversion and the crises of modernity are also the themes of le Fort's first Catholic novel, *The Veil of Veronica*, completed in Rome at the time of her reception into the Church. This novel rings with a spiritual melody that can enchant or alienate readers, much like its literary precedent, St. Thérèse of Lisieux's autobiographical *The Story of a Soul* (1898). As the memorable first-person narrator, Veronica, writes:

There exists for every human being a history of his life and a history of his soul, but there exists for each also a history of his soul with God. And this last, however curiously woven it may seem to be with the other two, is always at bottom a simple tale that follows its own straight path. For it is not so much a question of our fighting our way through to God, as of God fighting His way through to us.[12]

11. Le Fort, *Hymns to the Church*, 26.

12. Gertrud von le Fort, *The Veil of Veronica*, trans. Conrad M.R. Bonacina (Providence, RI: Cluny, 2019), 257.

Set in pre–World War 1 Rome, the novel depicts German émigrés sampling ancient and Christian cultures. The young Veronica is vulnerable—almost porous—to the personalities who compete to influence her. Her grandmother is a cheerful rationalist, exuberant in her conviction that reason has no need for faith. A young poet, Enzio, embodies the philosophical nihilism of Nietzsche and Rilke. In Enzio's poetry, the lights of both faith and reason are out. Veronica's Aunt Edelgart is a woman torn between the consolations of Christian faith and the consultations of Freudian psychology.

Both the city of Rome and the Church also play their parts in influencing Veronica, whose characteristic receptivity means she experiences deeply all the conflicting philosophies of life around her. The novel unfurls soulscapes against an unforgettable cityscape, careening from the desolate Colosseum by night to St. Peter's Basilica aflame with the Forty Hours' devotion. None among the great mid-century Catholic novels offers such an undaunted vocabulary for grace and its absence. Veronica experiences a terrible empathy as she imbibes Enzio's post-rational, post-Christian poetic vision. But this empathetic capacity also predisposes her to prayer. Kneeling before a crucifix, she will describe how:

> As if someone with lightning rapidity raised a curtain from my inmost soul, . . . I beheld there the self-same picture before which I knelt, like a stigma of love: received, denied, forgotten, and yet preserved intact because this love had preserved itself for me. From it alone had the call in my soul come: this same love, which had so often in front of the tabernacle drawn me to itself as to the source of all blessedness, now drew me to itself as if it had for my sake become pain.[13]

13. Le Fort, 266–267.

The Real Presence of the Redeemer, who is love, is more real than anything else in this novel. Its sacramental aesthetic will invite incredulous readers to suspend disbelief, while believing readers will find their spiritual vision extended by Veronica's sacramental sincerity.

VOCATION

The Crucified Christ as a vision of love that has become pain "for my sake": this image highlights a theological concept present in nearly all of le Fort's writing, namely, vicarious suffering. The nineteenth-century Marian apparitions at La Salette and Lourdes inspired a keen sense of what it means for the Christian to suffer, in union with Christ, for the sake of others. An older generation's habitual "offering up" of hardships was the pious expression of this theological reality: that, as St. Paul writes, we can "rejoice" in our sufferings for the sake of others because by this means we are "completing what is lacking in Christ's afflictions for the sake of his body, that is, the church" (Col. 1:24). The Catholic understanding of redemptive suffering animated le Fort's spirit and imagination. She drew deep from the well of Carmelite spirituality and likely considered a vocation to the religious life. "In Carmel," she wrote in 1935, "[the world] finds even what is most incomprehensible in its sufferings made worthy—through being offering up to Eternal Love—of being incorporated into participation in the redemptive suffering of the Cross."[14] These were the years of her friendship with Edith Stein, who would die in Auschwitz in 1942, living all this out—at the high pitch of sanctity. Stein had defined vicarious suffering in a letter written just before she entered Carmel in 1933:

14. Gertrud von le Fort, "Zu den Briefen in den Karmel: Marie Antoinette de Geuser," in *Aufzeichnungen und Erinnerungen* (Einsiedeln: Benziger Verlag, 1951), 51-52.

> There is a vocation to suffer with Christ and thereby to cooperate
> with him in his work of salvation. When we are united with the
> Lord, we are members of the mystical body of Christ: Christ
> lives on in his members and continues to suffer in them. And
> the suffering borne in union with the Lord is his suffering,
> incorporated in the great work of salvation and fruitful therein.[15]

The similarity between le Fort's and Stein's definitions of vicarious suffering is not coincidental. Each had come to understand her vocation through the fruitfulness of self-gift to the Crucified Christ. Le Fort would discern that her desire for religious life was more inclination than vocation, but her vocation as an artist remained anchored at the cross.

Examples of vicarious suffering proliferate in le Fort's fictions, most memorably in *The Song at the Scaffold* (1931). The novella tells a fictionalized account of the beatified Carmelites of Compiègne, who were guillotined late in the Reign of Terror in 1794. Le Fort knew that her story of religious persecution in revolutionary France had relevance to Weimar Germany, where Soviet Communism was feared and National Socialism was not feared enough. Le Fort inserts into history a fictional protagonist, Blanche de La Force. Thanks to the traumatic circumstances of her birth, Blanche worries her way into adulthood. Blanche's Enlightened father permits her entry into Carmel as a therapeutic salve to her chronic anxiety. Despite her sincere efforts, Blanche's religious vocation starts to look suspect. Is she trying to escape her fears? As revolution erupts outside the monastery, the sisters debate her suitability for religious life. The novice mistress, Sister Marie of the Incarnation, relishes the hint of martyrdom on the historic horizon and regards Blanche as a liability to the community. Like T.S. Eliot's Thomas à Becket in *Murder in the Cathedral*, Sister Marie risks a great error: she might commit "the greatest treason"—seek

---

15. Edith Stein, *Self-Portrait in Letters, 1916–42*, ed. Josephine Koeppel (Washington, DC: ICS, 1993), 128.

martyrdom—and "do the right deed for the wrong reason."[16] The meek prioress recognizes this temptation and sees in Blanche a mysterious calling. If the Carmelites are called to suffer for the sake of others, could this suffering take the form of anxiety and fear? Blanche is given the name in religion of Sister Blanche of Jesus in the Garden of Agony. The prioress recommends that she take "consolation in fear," "shelter in fear," even that she remain "loyal to fear." Le Fort is asking a difficult question to which her novella gives no unequivocal answer:

> Must fear and horror always be evil? Is it not possible that they may be deeper than courage, something that corresponds far more to the reality of things, to the terrors of the world, and to our own weakness?[17]

The novella touched a nerve at a nervous time. It found its way into many translations and, via the libretto of Georges Bernanos, inspired François Poulenc's powerful opera *Dialogues of the Carmelites* (1953–1956).

Writing fiction to pose tricky theological questions does not always generate the grittiest narratives. Reading le Fort's work is more like reading Caryll Houselander's guileless apologetics than Muriel Spark's snarky novels or Flannery O'Connor's hardcore short stories. But le Fort shares with these women an eye for the religious needs of the world around her. In *The Eternal Woman* (1934), she offers her "attempt to interpret the significance of woman, not according to her psychological or biological, her historical or social position, but under her symbolic aspect." Rejecting competing agendas, from socialist feminism to National Socialist biologism, le Fort laments that modernity has lost its

---

16. T.S. Eliot, *Murder in the Cathedral* (San Diego: Harcourt Brace, 1963), 44.

17. Gertrud von le Fort, *The Song at the Scaffold*, trans. Olga Marx (San Francisco: Ignatius, 2011), 28, 63, 32.

fluency in the "language of symbols." Without this language, she fears, we risk forgetting what we mean and who we are:

> Symbols are signs or images through which ultimate metaphysical realities and modes of being are apprehended, not in an abstract manner but by way of likeness. . . . The bearer may fall away from his symbol, but the symbol itself remains.

The Church's teaching about the woman who is Queen of Heaven and Mother of the Redeemer gives to all women a share in the paramount "metaphysical mystery of woman." Mary's *fiat* is the consummate act of surrender and cooperation in the work of redemption. "Creative power can only be received," writes le Fort. She sees this as a feminine capacity and corrective to the masculine impulse toward "self-redemption" and self-creation. Her understanding of Marian co-redemption is exemplary for men and women alike, who "must conceive the creative spirit in the sign of Mary, in humility and surrender, or he [and she] will not receive it at all." This explains le Fort's fascination with women's lives that have often been hidden in their creativity and importance. The occlusion of "half of reality" and "half of history" from the world stage, she believes, simply highlights the importance of things hidden and mysterious—from the gestating infant to contemplative prayer, from tragic suffering to disappointing failure. In this context, she discusses "spiritual motherhood," a concept that would be developed by Pope St. John Paul II in his apostolic letter *Mulieris Dignitatem* (1988). Le Fort's self-understanding as an artist derives from these reflections: "The invisible pillar of that which has come to pass must be rendered visible."[18] This sentence is key to interpreting many of le Fort's heroines, whose stories come fully to life only when

18. Gertrud von le Fort, *The Eternal Woman*, trans. Marie Cecilia Buehrle (San Francisco: Ignatius, 2010), 3, 18, 35.

who they are as persons coalesces with what they represent as symbols.[19]

REPARATION

Always opposed to National Socialism, le Fort's nostalgia for the medieval Holy Roman Empire under German tutelage led her into some naïve publications in the early 1930s. Unlike many prominent Jewish and other writers who were exiled after 1933, she remained in Germany, ranking among the "inner exiles," who wrote camouflaged critiques of the Third Reich.[20] Her works would soon be designated "undesirable"—though mostly still publishable—by organs of the regime. Her symbolic, sacramental view of history lent itself to this kind of writing against the grain of dictatorship. In the novel *The Wedding at Magdeburg* (1938) and the short story "The Ecstasy of the Maiden of Barby" (1940), she uses the Reformation and Counter-Reformation as historical foils to depict religious persecution and political mania. With less camouflage, she considers the intellectual rise of National Socialism in *The Wreath of Angels* (1946), a sequel to *The Veil of Veronica*. In 1944, she risked publishing part of this clumsy but fascinating commentary on Germany's submission to ideology only to have the print run destroyed in an air raid.

In 1946, le Fort would describe how terrifying visions of a post-Christian Germany haunted her during the Third Reich. She entertained questions that once seemed impossible: "What will remain if everything collapses? If, one day, the church doors close, the reception of the sacraments made impossible, the liturgy and pulpit fall silent, or if all our churches are reduced to rubble?" But she also offered an answer to her own bracing questions: "God will

19. See Ann Astell, "The Virgin Mary as Eternal Woman," *Church Life Journal*, December 10, 2018, https://churchlifejournal.nd.edu/articles/the-virgin-mary-as-eternal-woman/.

20. On the "inner exiles," see John Klapper, *Nonconformist Writing in Nazi Germany: The Literature of Inner Emigration* (Rochester, NY: Camden House, 2015).

remain with us, Christ, the Lord of the Church, even if all visible signs of his grace and all outward signs of his kingdom disappear." These are hard-won reflections, given le Fort's ecclesiological and sacramental vision of the world. They are not doubts about Christ's promises for his Church. But le Fort did foresee in those years a loneliness of faith that she could countenance only with deep trust in God's will and with a renewed "love for love."[21]

Although le Fort's late writing became more stylistically old-fashioned, she did her best to confront everything that Germans had to confront after the Holocaust. In *The Wife of Pilate* (1955), she imagines the anguish of the Roman woman who dreamed about Christ in Matthew 27 and is haunted by the merciful face of the mysterious Jewish prisoner. The woman later has another dream in which she realizes that her husband, Pontius Pilate, will be held guilty of Christ's death whenever the Creed is recited. Overwhelming personal and collective guilt—and the need for a spirit of reparation—is also the theme in *The Last Meeting* (1959) and *The Innocents* (1953).[22] Noteworthy among le Fort's late stories is *At the Gate of Heaven* (1954), which frames events surrounding the seventeenth-century trial of Galileo with the Allied bombings of Germany and the birth of the atomic age.[23] In Diana, a disciple of the Renaissance astronomer, le Fort shows how atheism seeds in disoriented minds and disappointed hearts. The story suggests that the mishandling of Galileo's scholarship by the Holy See unsettled the concord between faith and science, contributing to the rise of modern scientism. The story suggests that the reduction of all knowledge to science has accelerated technological progress but recklessly enabled the worst atrocities of modern history. Divine mercy is a unifying thread in these

21. Gertrud von le Fort, *Unser Weg durch die Nacht* (Wiesbaden: Insel, 1950), 13–15.

22. In Gertrud von le Fort, *The Innocents and Other Stories*, trans. Michael J. Miller (San Francisco: Ignatius, 2019).

23. In Gertrud von le Fort, *The Wife of Pilate and Other Stories*, trans. Michael J. Miller (San Francisco: Ignatius, 2015).

stories from the post-war years. And vicarious suffering, the oldest preoccupation in le Fort's Catholic fiction, gained devastating relevance amid the reckonings of the post-Nazi period.

Readers may find the simplicity of faith evident in these post-war works inadequate to the dire historical facts they address. But le Fort's guileless imagination remained beguiling to the end. In a series of late poems, she gives thanks for her vocation as a writer. Art came to her "unbidden," overwhelming her in a manner she can compare only to grace. The melancholic, middle-aged baroness who, between two world wars, worried about the second half of her life can now only wonder at its gifts. "How glorious it is," she writes, "to depend on a heavenly voice." The poet, she affirms, is *christverwandt*—kindred to Christ.[24] Here is a writer who clings undauntedly to her pen as she seeks to cling, undauntedly, to him.

RECOMMENDED READING

Gertrud von le Fort. *The Eternal Woman.*
_____. *Hymns to the Church.*
_____. *The Innocents and Other Stories.*
_____. *The Song at the Scaffold.*
_____. *The Veil of Veronica.*
_____. *The Wife of Pilate and Other Stories.*

Helena M. Tomko is associate professor of literature in the Department of Humanities at Villanova University. She has published widely on German Catholic culture in the Weimar Republic and Third Reich. Her new book project explores why so many of the best Catholic fictions are funny. This literary study will also offer a theory of sacramental humor and the cheerfulness of Christian life.

24. Gertrud von le Fort, *Gedichte* (Wiesbaden: Insel, 1958), 1, 9, 11.

Flannery O'Connor: Incarnational Fiction

Angela Alaimo O'Donnell

If there were a poster girl for great Catholic women writers, Flannery O'Connor would be her. A faithful Catholic from cradle to grave, a daily communicant for much of her adult life, a deep reader of Catholic philosophy and theology, and an award-winning writer who, during her brief time on earth—and beyond—earned accolades and the fandom of contemporary readers and critics, both Catholic and otherwise, for her signature, heart-stopping, hilarious and horrific, grotesque, and powerful storytelling, O'Connor is the reigning queen of American Catholic writers, as well as one of the finest writers of the twentieth century—a distinction few Catholic writers can claim.

FLANNERY O'CONNOR AS CATHOLIC WRITER

There are many reasons for O'Connor's appeal to readers of many stamps, and one of them is that in her fiction O'Connor does not wear her religion on her sleeve. In fact, it is very easy to read O'Connor's work and not even know she is a Catholic. Her stories and novels do not feature what we might term Catholic content and rarely contain Catholic characters. As a writer, O'Connor is not out to convert the reader to her faith. Rather, her vocation is to live "hotly in pursuit of the real" and to convey that reality, as she sees it, to the reader.[1] Of course, even a cursory knowledge of her biography demonstrates that O'Connor was a Catholic—and a serious one at that—and once a reader makes this discovery, the thumb prints of her faith appear all over the pages of her books. Thus, her work is of great interest to lovers of literature and also to a growing number of readers in search of writers who consciously explore the intersection between art and faith.

In her essays and her letters, O'Connor writes eloquently about her vocation as an artist. Few writers are as self-aware as Flannery O'Connor in terms of what she is trying to accomplish in her fiction and what distinguishes her work from that of her contemporaries. She states in one of her essays, quoting her favorite theologian,

> St. Thomas Aquinas says that art ... is wholly concerned with the good of that which is made. He says that a work of art is a good in itself, and this is a truth that the modern world has largely forgotten. We are not content to stay within our limitations and make something that is simply a good in and by itself. Now we want to make something that will have some utilitarian value. Yet what is good in itself glorifies God because it reflects God. The artist has his hands full and does his duty if he attends to his art. He can safely leave evangelizing to the evangelists.[2]

As an artist, O'Connor's primary commitment is to her craft, storytelling—a craft that is certainly informed by her identity and formation as a Catholic, for the writer writes with "the whole personality" but is not limited by it.[3] Contrary to the popular

1. Flannery O'Connor, *Mystery and Manners: Occasional Prose*, ed. Robert and Sally Fitzgerald (New York: Farrar, Straus and Giroux, 1970), 171.

2. O'Connor, 171.

3. O'Connor, 181.

perception of the secular culture she writes for, her religious identity and the perspective it provides does not circumscribe her vision: "The Christian novelist lives in a larger universe. He believes that the natural world contains the supernatural. And this doesn't mean that his obligation to portray the natural is less; it means it is greater."[4] As with many other Catholic writers, O'Connor's work features a devotion to what philosopher William F. Lynch, SJ (another of O'Connor's favorite writers) refers to as "the definite."[5] Christ is the symbol of the definite, the limited, the particular, the real, and the Christic imagination is one that traffics in the real. O'Connor states this idea in her characteristically concrete way, reminding us that "Christ didn't redeem us by a direct intellectual act, but became incarnate in human form, and he speaks to us now through the mediation of the visible Church. All this may seem a long way from the subject of fiction, but it is not, for the main concern of the fiction writer is with mystery as it is incarnated in human life."[6] O'Connor's emphasis on the word "incarnate" here attests to her focus on the Christian concept of the Incarnation, both in terms of its theological importance in the Judeo-Christian schema of salvation and also in terms of the ways that her work as a seer and a writer embraces and embodies the concept. O'Connor's storytelling is radically incarnational in its attempt to enflesh the truths of the invisible, eternal universe through her portrayal of visible, mundane reality. And that reality is vivid and violent.

In her two novels and thirty-one short stories, O'Connor takes the reader places we do not expect to go. We encounter radically flawed people, many of them in possession of physical and emotional afflictions that indicate a troubled and troubling spiritual disposition. A number of O'Connor's characters are grotesques: human beings who model extreme appearances and

4. O'Connor, 175.

5. William F. Lynch, *Christ and Apollo* (Washington, DC: ISI Books, 1960), 5.

6. O'Connor, *Mystery and Manners*, 176.

behaviors that exaggerate our own tendencies and afflictions in order to make them more visible and obvious to the reader. Numbered among her characters are serial killers, pyromaniacs, child-murderers, rapists, one-legged philosophers, one-armed conmen, intellectually disabled children, false prophets, and mean grandparents. These are the "folks" (to use O'Connor's word) who people her fiction and who people her world. Many of her characters can also be seen as "freaks," another term she used to capture the uniqueness of the human personality, the incarnational fact that people are imperfect and misshapen in their own peculiar ways. The one thing that binds all of these strange and disparate people together is the fact that all are in need of conversion or radical change: "All of my stories are about the operation of Grace on a character who is not very willing to support it," she writes in one of her letters.[7] The events that befall them are generally sudden, shocking, and violent occurrences that wake them up to their human flaws and weaknesses and demonstrate their moral blindness, their besetting sins, and their need to change their lives.

Violence is a trademark of O'Connor's fiction and is a deliberate and necessary element of her stories for several reasons. First, as a Catholic writing for secular readers, "an audience that is unprepared and unwilling to see the meaning of life as [s]he sees it," O'Connor admits that the writer must sometimes "resort to violent literary means" to get her vision across. "You have to make your vision apparent by shock—to the hard of hearing you shout, and for the almost blind you draw large startling figures."[8] In addition, the violence that befalls her characters is necessary to their salvation: "In my own stories I have found that violence is strangely capable of returning my characters to reality and preparing them to accept their moment of grace. Their heads are

7. Flannery O'Connor, *The Habit of Being* (New York: Farrar, Straus and Giroux, 1988), 275.

8. O'Connor, *Mystery and Manners*, 184, 34.

so hard that almost nothing else will do the work. This idea, that reality is something to which we must be returned at considerable cost, is one which is seldom understood by the casual reader, but it is one which is implicit in the Christian view of the world."[9] This idea of violence as a means to grace is quintessential O'Connor—and one that sometimes gets her into trouble. Some readers have found (and continue to find) her work disturbing and unnerving. O'Connor's response to this objection was, essentially, "Good!" Art is supposed to disturb and unnerve, to rock the reader, to shock her out of her complacency, and to help open her up for her own revelation of grace. O'Connor once wrote, "You can't clobber any reader while he's looking. You divert his attention, then you clobber him and he never knows what hit him."[10] And clobbered we are. O'Connor's plots are famously chilling. Terrible things happen to ordinary people, and we, the readers, bear witness to the human struggle to endure the unendurable and, sometimes, watch them emerge triumphant.

THE LIFE OF FLANNERY O'CONNOR

It behooves us to explore some of O'Connor's stories in some detail, but first it seems necessary to retell the story of O'Connor's life and to see what connections there might be between this brilliant, odd, shy, wry woman from rural Georgia and the mighty stories she wrote.

In one of her letters, Flannery O'Connor frankly (and mistakenly) predicts, "There won't be any biographies of me, for only one reason, lives spent between the house and the chicken yard do not make for exciting copy."[11] O'Connor knew a good story when she read—and wrote—one. Given this, it is ironic, perhaps, that she did not see the drama and grandeur of her own. While it is

9. O'Connor, 112.

10. O'Connor, *Habit of Being*, 202.

11. O'Connor, 290–291.

true that the details of her life do not constitute tabloid fare, it is the quiet ordinariness of her story that makes it remarkable.

The outline of her life is spare, elegant, and easily traceable. Born in Savannah on March 25, 1925 (the Feast of the Annunciation), Flannery was christened Mary Flannery O'Connor by her parents, Regina Cline and Edward F. O'Connor, both observant Catholics. She would later drop the "Mary" and use her middle name instead as a more fitting—and memorable—pen name for a writer than that of "an Irish washerwoman."[12]

Mary Flannery grew up an only child under their watchful eye in the fashionable section of the Irish Catholic ghetto of Savannah. She attended parochial school and was educated by the Sisters of Mercy. However, her Catholic education was an experience she did not particularly enjoy: Mary Flannery didn't quite fit in with the demure, obedient schoolgirls of Savannah. In addition, she didn't much care for the nuns who taught her, many of whom were very young, "just off the boat" from Ireland. She was cleverer than most of them, and she knew it. Young Flannery's resistance to traditional education was an early sign of her nonconformity and her radically original view of the world. For instance, she refused to learn how to spell—a habit that persisted into her adulthood. (She would refer to herself hereafter as "an innocent speller.") In the writing that was required of her, she would insist upon writing about birds—chickens and ducks, in particular—obsessively. This obsession with birds marked her, in the nuns' eyes, as a child who wasn't very bright. It would remain with her throughout her life, leading eventually to the extravagant collection of peacocks she amassed while living on Andalusia farm.

When Flannery was an adolescent, the family moved to Milledgeville, where most of her mother's large family, the Clines, lived. Catholics in rural Georgia at that time (1938) were rare, and

12. Quoted in Richard Gilman, "On Flannery O'Connor," *The New York Review*, August 21, 1969.

among the few Catholic families there, the Clines/O'Connors were unusually prosperous, thus setting them apart from their own kind. This, in addition to Flannery's identity as an only child, marked her out for a solitary childhood and a semi-solitary adolescence, one she spent among affectionate, attentive adults. Her reasonably happy childhood, however, came to an end suddenly at age fifteen when her father—whom she adored—died from lupus, a heredity disease that would, eventually, afflict Flannery and cause her premature death at age thirty-nine.

O'Connor remained in Milledgeville, close to family, attending Georgia State College for Women, where she earned a bachelor's degree in social sciences. After her graduation, the world opened up for O'Connor when she went to graduate school at the Iowa Writer's Workshop, where she encountered influential writers who would admire and help promote her work. As a result of these connections, O'Connor would move to New York City, the center of the writing and publishing world, and eventually take up residence in Connecticut with poet, translator, and scholar Robert Fitzgerald and his wife, Sally, Catholic literary friends introduced to her by their mutual friend, poet Robert Lowell. The Fitzgeralds provided O'Connor with both physical and intellectual space wherein her writing would flourish. They offered fellowship and friendship that would last the rest of her life, and after her death they would generously promote her work, editing and publishing O'Connor's essays and letters, invaluable documents for her readers for generations to come. Just as O'Connor seemed poised on the brink of success—having completed her first novel, *Wise Blood*, and found a publisher at age twenty-five—the diagnosis of lupus sent her back to Georgia, back to the family farm she knew as a child that bore the exotic name "Andalusia," and back to a state of childlike dependency, as she would live with her mother, Regina, who cared for her in her debilitating sickness until she died.

It was during her thirteen-year exile at Andalusia that she spent her days, as described in her letters, divided between the house and the kitchen yard. From her vantage point, her life was "as ordinary as a loaf of bread," as O.E. Parker in her story "Parker's Back" says of himself. This statement is surely an expression of O'Connor's humility and perhaps a manifestation of her disappointment. She saw little in her own life that would lead to fame or fortune, so she had to content herself with obscurity—or so she thought.

O'Connor's earthly pilgrimage was brief and poignant. We are moved by her life, her death, and the particulars of her journey in part because through her stories, essays, and letters, readers get to know her extraordinarily well. During the time when O'Connor was living her quiet life at Andalusia, she was corresponding with friends and fellow writers, publishers, readers, and fans of her work. Reading these letters, we become eavesdroppers, overhearing stories of every kind, ranging from her delight in the peafowl she raises to her pleasure at meeting a quirky couple at the doctor's office who inspire some of her own characters; from her steely disapproval of the suggestions made by an editor regarding a piece of her work to her enthusiastic admiration of her favorite writers; from profound theological insights she gains from her reading to the generous spiritual direction she provides for correspondents who write to her about matters of faith. We also bear witness to O'Connor's courage, gratitude, and irrepressible grace in the face of the disease that is slowly and inexorably ravaging her body. By the time death arrives on August 3, 1964, the reader feels very much as if he or she has lost a friend and fellow-traveling companion along the pilgrimage of life.

During her time at Andalusia, O'Connor's writing became her lifeline. Her fiction gave her a reason for enduring, and she wrote every morning (two hours was all she could manage) despite the painful and debilitating effects of both the disease and the medications prescribed to remedy it. She became an avid observer of her circumscribed world. With her eye for detail and her fine ear for idiom, she watched and listened to her neighbors and to the farm workers, who would provide models for her of the white farmers and sharecroppers and the African-American laborers who people her stories. She would also study the newspapers for interesting (and sometimes wild) local stories, scenarios, and names of characters. What seemed like a place of exile would prove to be the source of her inspiration. She acknowledged later in life, "The best of my writing has been done here."[13]

FLANNERY O'CONNOR'S FICTION

Flannery O'Connor's literary legacy is a rich one. The fact that she made her mark before she was forty years old and on the strength of a comparatively small output (compared with the likes of more prolific and long-lived writers, such as fellow Southern novelist William Faulkner) is remarkable. One explanation for this is the total uniqueness of her work. O'Connor's mastery of her chosen terrain—the grotesqueness of her characters, the blending of the tragic and the comic, her unerring ear for the idiom of Southern speech, and her relentless exploration of the human tendency toward sin and the need for grace—gives her work an urgency, eccentricity, and signature charm that makes it instantly recognizable as hers. It is also noteworthy that though O'Connor produced two powerful novels, *Wise Blood* and *The Violent Bear It Away* (plus portions of a third left unfinished at her death, titled *Why Do The Heathen Rage?*), she is most lauded for her expert and unparalleled achievement in the thirty-one short stories she wrote. One of many signs of the literary world's recognition of O'Connor's mastery of the genre is the fact that *The Complete Stories of Flannery O'Connor*, published in 1971, received the coveted National Book Award in 1972, eight years after O'Connor's death, marking the first time the prize was awarded to a writer posthumously.

13. Flannery O'Connor, *Collected Works* (New York: Library of America, 1988), 1037.

"A Good Man is Hard to Find"

O'Connor's most famous short story, and perhaps her most noto-rious, "A Good Man is Hard to Find" demonstrates the power of her work and the excellence of her craft. (Fair warning to readers: spoilers follow.) The plot unfolds with astonishing speed, taking the characters (and readers) on the ride of their life. A chatty old grandma tries to convince her family not to go to Florida on vacation. There is a serial killer, who calls himself the Misfit, on the loose. Nonetheless, the family goes. Along the journey, she convinces them to leave the main road to see an abandoned mansion she recalls from her childhood. Unfortunately, the grandmother misremembers, and instead of the grand mansion they come face to face with the mass murderer she so dreaded. The Misfit's henchmen take the family members into the woods, one by one, and shoot them, until only the grandmother is left. She tries to convince the Misfit to pray and mend his ways. When she reaches out to touch him, he shoots her three times in the chest. The last we see of the grandmother, she is lying in a ditch in a puddle of blood, looking up at the sky, and smiling. The Misfit offers a brief eulogy: "She would have been a good woman if it had been somebody there to shoot her every minute of her life."[14]

As the story unfolds, it is, admittedly, hard to watch, but, as with a wreck on the side of the road, it is impossible to look away. One of the most disturbing things about this story—and a signature of O'Connor's style—is the commingling of the com-edy of everyday life and unspeakable horror. The story is full of humorous observations, often at the expense of the characters, revealing their foolishness and vanity. As readers we find ourselves laughing in spite of ourselves, even as some of the story's most dis-turbing events are occurring. For example, the fact that the grand-mother's adult son, Bailey, is wearing a festive yellow button-down

14. Flannery O'Connor, *The Complete Stories* (New York: Farrar, Straus and Giroux, 1971), 133.

shirt absurdly decorated with bright blue parrots during these grim proceedings, and the fact that the Misfit appropriates the shirt and wears it even as he shoots the grandmother, is a piece of dark comedy. The grotesque discrepancy between the seriousness of the action and the playfulness of the clothing is both shocking and real. *This is not how serial killers dress!* the reader thinks—*or is it?* For O'Connor, as for Shakespeare and every writer who attempts to create a realistic vision, comedy and tragedy cannot be separated: life consists of a messy pastiche of both. O'Connor once wrote, "Either one is serious about salvation or one is not. And it is well to realize that the maximum amount of seriousness admits the maximum amount of comedy. Only if we are secure in our beliefs can we see the comical side of the universe."[15] Implicit in her creation of characters in need of conversion, her use of violence as a means to grace, and her mingling of the comic and the tragic is O'Connor's deeply Catholic vision, one that sees the possibility of redemption available to humanity in all places, in all times, and through the most unexpected of means.

In O'Connor's world, grace manifests itself in the most unlikely people and places. As in life, the Lord does indeed work in mysterious ways. In this particular story, saving grace arrives for the grandmother in the person of a mass murderer. Her gesture of reaching out to the Misfit in a rare moment of compassion and self-forgetfulness is likely the finest thing this petty, shallow woman has ever done. His response, of course, is to deflect her gesture of goodness and answer it with evil, but in O'Connor's spiritual economy, the grandmother's soul has been saved. The old woman dies, but she dies happy and she dies well, not trembling and begging for her life but comforting a fellow human being. To invoke a scriptural passage O'Connor knew well, sometimes one must lose one's life to find it. In addition to the grandmother's salvation, there is also the implication at the end

15. O'Connor, *Mystery and Manners*, 167.

of the story that the Misfit has been changed by his encounter with the grandmother. In the very last line of the story, he denies his previous claim that murder and mayhem are fun, that there's "no pleasure but in meanness," when he tells one of his henchmen, "It's no real pleasure in life."[16] O'Connor confirms the Misfit's incipient conversion in one of her essays: "I don't want to equate the Misfit with the devil. I prefer to think that, however unlikely this may seem, the old lady's gesture, like the mustard seed, will grow to be a great crow-filled tree in the Misfit's heart, and will be enough of a pain to him there to turn him into the prophet he was meant to become. But that's another story."[17] A key element of O'Connor's Catholicism that shows up in story after story is the generosity of God's mercy. No one is exempt from the possibility of grace, redemption, and salvation. Not even serial killers.

"Revelation"

Another signature story by O'Connor is "Revelation," one of the last stories she wrote and one of her most powerful. "Revelation" is remarkable in O'Connor's *oeurve* for a number of reasons, and one such reason is that O'Connor takes on the subject of the sin of racism. Ruby Turpin, the main protagonist in "Revelation," is one of O'Connor's larger-than-life women, in every sense of the term. Physically large and imposing, she takes up a lot of room in the tiny doctor's office, where the reader first meets her, along with her husband, Claud, but she also takes up a lot of psychic space. Mrs. Turpin fancies herself a connoisseur of humanity, casting her eye about the place, sizing up her fellow human beings, and judging their worth based on their cleanliness, appearance, speech, and, most notably, their shoes. Possessed of a kind of rage for social order, Mrs. Turpin would go to sleep at night, categorizing people according to a rigid hierarchy in terms of

16. O'Connor, *Complete Stories*, 132, 133.
17. O'Connor, *Mystery and Manners*, 112–113.

race and class. "On the bottom of the heap were most colored people . . . then next to them—not above, just away from—were the white-trash." However, gradually the complexity of trying to find the right place for everyone in her imagined hierarchy of human value would bear in on her: "Usually by the time she had fallen asleep all the classes of people were moiling and roiling around in her head, and she would dream they were all crammed in together in a box car, being ridden off to be put in a gas oven."[18]

Mrs. Turpin is both a racist and a bigot—identities she is blissfully ignorant of—and owing to this lack of self-knowledge, she also believes she is "saved," in the Southern Protestant lingo of her place and era. She does not recognize the darkness of her own dreams, the image of the box cars and gas ovens echoing the Holocaust, the embodiment of another murderous culture with a rage for social order. Instead, she congratulates herself on her piety, publicly professing her love of Jesus, singing along to the Gospel songs on the radio, and thanking God for having made her such a good person. She sees no contradiction between her contempt for other human beings and her identity as a Christian.

Mrs. Turpin bears all the marks of an O'Connor character who is sorely in need of a wakeup call. Unaware of her spiritual peril, too blinded by her own (supposed) virtues to see her sins, it will take some sort of shocking, violent event to dislodge her from her complacent state and force her to see herself as she truly is. That event comes, reliably and in the nick of time, in the form of a book, titled *Human Development*, hurled across the room by a homely young woman named Mary Grace, Ruby Turpin's nemesis. Mrs. Turpin has seen the girl reading her book and glancing up often to eye her with fierce contempt, but she could not possibly understand why the young woman might have conceived such a virulent hatred for her. After the girl strikes her with the book, just above her left eye, Mrs. Turpin's vision is immediately altered.

18. O'Connor, *Complete Stories*, 491.

At first, the room and all the people in it seem small and distant, and then her vision reverses itself so everything appears larger than it is. The world no longer seems as certain as it did before. Instinctively, Mrs. Turpin feels as if the girl knows her in some essential way and has a message to deliver: "What you got to say to me?" she asks and waits, holding her breath "as for a revelation." The girl's response to this woman of supposed virtue is stunning: "Go back to hell where you came from, you old wart hog."[19]

Mrs. Turpin may be a racist and a bigot, but even she (like any other sinner) is not beyond redemption. The aptly named Mary Grace has delivered a disturbing but potentially salvific annunciation to Mrs. Turpin, and she is haunted by it for the remainder of the story. She cannot rest without seeing the image of the hog, an unredeemed and biblically unclean creature, as a version of herself, casting her in a new light wherein all of her ugliness is suddenly evident. In her confusion and rage, she tries to share the message with Claud, but she cannot bear to have her beloved husband think of her this way; she tries to share it with the black field workers employed on her farm, but they refuse to take Mrs. Turpin's distress seriously and treat her with the mock sympathy and comic condescension she deserves. In the end, she takes her case directly to God. Walking across the fields toward the hogs, creatures she must wash and feed and keep alive, "She had the look of a woman going single-handed, weaponless, into battle."[20] In the light of the setting sun (wherein O'Connor invokes the identity between the sun and the Son), she interrogates God and demands answers: "How am I a hog and me both?" Mrs. Turpin's view, until now, has been too schematic, as her faulty class system would suggest, too black and white. One is either good or evil, saved or damned, a sinner or a saint—such theology makes no allowances for human complexity, the role of saving grace, and the mercy of God. Her soliloquy culminates

19. O'Connor, 500.
20. O'Connor, 505.

in a final surge of fury that shakes her as she roars, "Who do you think you are?"[21]

The answer Mrs. Turpin receives is threefold. First, she is given a glimpse of the fragility of human life, as she sees her husband's truck tooling along in the distance, dwarfed by the horizon, and vulnerable to accident. Next, she senses the mystery of the world she inhabits, one that is suffused with divine presence. Even the pigs in the pen before her "pant with a secret life." Mrs. Turpin, large as she is, realizes how small and vulnerable the individual human person is and how dependent upon God all creatures are. And then, in one final, fantastic, visionary moment, she is granted a vision of the heavenly procession of the communion of saints:

> She saw the streak [in the sky] as a vast swinging bridge extending upward from the earth through a field of living fire. Upon it a vast horde of souls were rumbling toward heaven. There were whole companies of white-trash, clean for the first time in their lives, and bands of black n----- in white robes, and battalions of freaks and lunatics shouting and clapping and leaping like frogs. And bringing up the end of the procession was a tribe of people whom she recognized at once as those who, like herself and Claud, had always had a little of everything and the God-given wit to use it right. She learned forward to observe them closer. They were marching behind the others with great dignity, accountable as they had always been for good order and common sense and respectable behavior. They alone were on key. Yet she could see by their shocked and altered faces that even their virtues were being burned away.[22]

Mrs. Turpin's vision is a clear corrective to the coarse classification system she had lived by, to her bigoted view of blacks and poor whites, the disabled, the insane, and all other human beings

21. O'Connor, 506, 507.
22. O'Connor, 508.

she thought were beneath her. To the contrary, the hierarchy is flipped, and the heavenly procession is a concrete embodiment of the biblical maxim "the last shall be first." While these—the sinned-against, the marginalized, and the dispossessed—are much beloved of God and received first into the kingdom, the self-righteous and supposedly virtuous bring up the rear. The good news is there is a place for them in the kingdom; the bad news, for Mrs. Turpin, is that the place is not nearly as august as she had imagined.

At the end of the story, Mrs. Turpin is utterly altered. The message of Mary Grace and the vision she conjures enables her to see her sinful nature and her true place in the schema of salvation. What's more, this knowledge arrives in sufficient time to enable her to amend her ways, to at least attempt to give up her hasty judgments and petty hatreds, and to live a good life—an opportunity the grandmother in "A Good Man is Hard to Find" did not have. Grace has been extended to her, and she has embraced it.

The number of words written about Flannery O'Connor's work outnumbers by a large measure the number of words that O'Connor herself wrote. Given her wry sense of humor and her humility, O'Connor would almost certainly find this amusing. It is also a testament to the outsized influence O'Connor has had, and continues to have, on the generations of readers and writers before us and those to come.

RECOMMENDED READING

Flannery O'Connor. *The Complete Stories.* (Begin with "A Good Man Is Hard to Find" and "Revelation.")
_____. *The Habit of Being.*
_____. *Mystery and Manners: Occasional Prose.*
_____. *The Violent Bear It Away.*
_____. *Wise Blood.*

Angela Alaimo O'Donnell is a professor, poet, literary critic, and writer at Fordham University in New York City. She also serves as Associate Director of Fordham's Curran Center for American Catholic Studies. Her publications include the award-winning biography *Flannery O'Connor: Fiction Fired by Faith* (2015); *The Province of Joy* (2012), a book of hours based on the practical theology of Flannery O'Connor; *Radical Ambivalence: Race in Flannery O'Connor* (2020), the first book-length study of O'Connor and race; and *Andalusian Hours* (2020), a collection of 101 poems that channel the voice of Flannery O'Connor. She is currently at work on a follow-up book to her previous study *The Whole Story: Flannery O'Connor, Race, & the Prophetic Imagination.*

Caroline Gordon:
Lost and Found

Joshua Hren

More than midway through the journey of her life, Caroline Gordon (1895–1981) converted to the Catholic faith. "I was nearly fifty year's old before I discovered that art is the handmaiden of the Church," she wrote in her 1964 essay "Letters to a Monk."[1] She'd become a handmaiden of literature far younger. Having received an unconventional classical education at her father's Clarksville School for Boys, she would win a Guggenheim and an O. Henry Prize and mingle familiarly with not a few of the twentieth century's literary lodestars: Hemingway and Faulkner, F. Scott Fitzgerald and her mentor Ford Madox Ford, not to mention her (handful of a) husband, the distinguished (later Catholic) critic and poet Allen Tate. She and Tate began as Greenwich Village bohemians, and by the time City Hall handed them a marriage certificate in 1925, Caroline was already five months pregnant with their first child. The wedding commenced not bliss but the bitterness born of a husband bent on courting and chasing other women. In January of 1946 she granted Tate the divorce he requested, only to reconcile with and remarry him in April.

---

1. Caroline Gordon, "Letters to a Monk," *Ramparts* 3 (December 1964): 4–10.

Gordon became Catholic in 1947, on the feast of St. John of the Cross, and the remainder of her marital life would be marked by many dark nights of the soul. For though the gates of hell do not prevail against the Church, her entrance into St. Peter's barque brought not rest but what Anne M. Boyle describes as "years of bitter separations and appeasements," and many decades of the Rosary could not stave off their final divorce a little over a decade after Tate's litany of afflictive affairs.[2] If marriage is meant to be a sacramental analogy of the perfect Trinity's triangular *agápē*, it is no wonder that the route Gordon took to the faith assumed a more complex and rough-edged shape.

Her conversion came about from a confluence of causes. Paul Elie argues that turnings toward the Church was something of a trend among the Lost Generation's artists, directionless and adrift after the First World War's chaos, who sought "an otherworldly ideal" in the solid mystical solace of the Church.[3] Witness such a turning in the Pulitzer Prize–winning poet Robert Lowell (who camped, for a time, on Gordon's lawn), Harlem Renaissance writer Claude McKay (whose pendulum swung from Communism to Catholicism), and a number of other notables. Gordon alternately cited the Gospel of St. Mark and the *Bhagavad Gita* as some of the sources that showed her—straightforwardly or circuitously—the truth of the faith. And last, but maybe first in terms of motivating forces, she'd struck up a friendship with Servant of God Dorothy Day during her stay in New York, and the radical Catholic's duty of delight showed her that sanctity need not be bourgeois or stuffy but could set off the Roman Church's candle even in the gutters and breadlines of the NYC Bowery. "The only people for me," said the sometimes-Catholic Jack Kerouac, "are the mad ones, the ones who are mad to live, mad to talk, mad to be saved . . . the ones who

2. Anne M. Boyle, *Strange and Lurid Bloom: A Study of the Fiction of Caroline Gordon* (Madison, NJ: Fairleigh Dickinson University Press, 2002), 169.

3. Paul Elie, *The Life You Save May Be Your Own: An American Pilgrimage* (New York: Farrar, Straus and Giroux, 2004), 111.

never yawn or say a commonplace thing, but burn, burn, burn like fabulous yellow roman candles exploding like spiders across the stars."[4] Such fervent sentiments could have fallen from the lips of Gordon's own Lost Generation protagonists, so many of whom are dying to be found by the Hound of Heaven.

When her importance is recalled at all, Caroline Gordon is typically reckoned as wife of Tate and indispensable editor and mentor of many. Who knows? Without her rallying praise and exacting advice, Walker Percy may never have gotten out from under his burned early novel *The Charterhouse*, and *The Moviegoer* may have remained an existentialist *essai* (a "try" or "attempt") rather than a National Book Award recipient.

When the Catholic publisher Robert Giroux wavered over Flannery O'Connor's first novel *Wise Blood,* the great Harvard classicist Robert Fitzgerald asked Gordon to apply her sharpened sensibilities to the manuscript, which the author came to call "Opus Nauseous No.1." Gordon immediately recognized that "this girl is a real novelist" and wrote to the young talent a long letter filled with earnest appreciations ("There are so few Catholics who seem possessed of a literary conscience") and painstaking criticisms ("I don't think that your title is prepared for enough") that gave the novel a needed transfusion.[5] O'Connor was not oblivious to the "great pains" that her elder took; she remained overwhelmed by Gordon's "very generous" criticism and her "highly energetic and violently enthusiastic" acumen, even as her adept mentor made her "feel like [an] illiterate grandmother."[6]

In spite of this awesome arc of influence, Gordon's own fiction has remained, in the main, untouched. A number of her novels, long out of print, have been lost to prospective generations of

4. Jack Kerouac, *On The Road: The Original Scroll* (New York: Penguin, 2008), 113.

5. Christine Flanagan, ed., *The Letters of Flannery O'Connor and Caroline Gordon* (Athens, GA: University of Georgia Press, 2018), 1, 22, 27.

6. Flanagan, 11.

readers. Of late Gordon has been "found" again. In the last few years, we have seen the publication of *The Letters of Flannery O'Connor and Caroline Gordon*, edited by Christine Flanagan. In *Good Things Out of Nazareth* (whose title is taken from Gordon's own description of the Southern Catholic literary movement), Gordon plays a major part. And, finally, Cluny Media, as part of its sustained push to bring many "Catholic novels" back into print, has republished three of Gordon's important works: *How to Read a Novel*, *The Malefactors*, and *The House of Fiction*.

Gordon wrote two novels in the years immediately following her fullness of communion with the Church. Although the fiction she penned post-conversion is obsessed with her characters' salvation or damnation, and she frequently holds up eccentric saints as electrifying moral centers of her novels, James E. Rocks is correct to write that her "Catholics may not be good representatives of religion . . . because their feet are too obviously made of clay."[7] Their graspings after God are convoluted and concomitant with what St. John Henry Newman described as fiction's strong suit: a record of man in rebellion. *The Strange Children*, published the same year as *Wise Blood* (1952), was nominated for the National Book Award alongside works by J.D. Salinger and Truman Capote. *The Malefactors*, which followed four years later and came out as a Cluny Classic in 2019, is a novel of the "Lost Generation." Although the protagonists Tom and Vera Claiborne inhabit the headquarters of "a party every day" at their farm at Blencker's Bridge, the novel is mainly a portrait of a strained marriage saved.[8] The odds of this "strange book" (to cite the original jacket cover) were undermined before it reached readers' hands. Gordon had originally dedicated the work to Dorothy Day, who is fictionally refracted in the character Catherine Pollard. Day was astonished to find herself rendered, in Paul Elie's words, "as a holy seductress

---

7. James E. Rocks, "The Christian Myth as Salvation: Caroline Gordon's 'The Strange Children,'" in *Tulane Studies in English* 16 (1968): 149–160.

8. Caroline Gordon, *The Malefactors* (Providence, RI: Cluny, 2019), 19.

with a blasphemous past"—including participation in a Black Mass.[9] Although Gordon considered the book as "a tribute, an act of devotion," Day wrote "forceful letters" demanding that the "To Dorothy Day," as well as her character's dabbling in Satanism, be exorcised.[10]

As Bainard Cheney notes, "The decision, just before publication, to eliminate the dedication, gave the publisher cold feet, and the novel was shelved rather than promoted: perhaps a considerable reason for its small sale."[11] Fifteen years after its initial appearance, Cheney tried to champion the novel back into print. He cited *Collier's Encyclopedia* entry for 1956, which registered *The Malefactors* as "probably the finest novel of the year—in certain respects if not in all."[12] He summoned the strength of Arthur Mizener's *New York Times* review, which insisted that "her books have grown more skillful with time" even as "not many people seem to notice. The decades go on tossing up their temporary immortals . . . and Miss Gordon goes on being unnoticed."[13] Let's do some noticing: let's try to rightly situate her stature.

Gordon joined the ranks of Dostoevsky in striving to write saints; specifically, she sought to transpose the great Catholic Worker founders Peter Maurin and Dorothy Day into compelling figures charged with captivating sanctity. "She certainly had a hard time making those CW [Catholic Worker] people believable," O'Connor confessed, reluctantly conceding her elder's limitations.[14] That these characters make for some of the weakest portraits in the book does not first reflect Gordon's incapacity as an artist so much as it manifests a perennial problem for writers

9. Paul Elie, *The Life You Save May Be Your Own*, 238.

10. Elie, 238.

11. Brainard Cheney, "Caroline Gordon's 'The Malefactors,'" *The Sewanee Review* 79, no. 3 (1971): 360–372.

12. Cheney, 360.

13. Cheney, 360.

14. Paul Elie, *The Life You Save May Be Your Own*, 240.

striving to advance what Sister Mariella Gable, OSB, calls a compelling "psychology of goodness" that could move "the reader to accept the good as lovable . . . with anything like artistic success that commonly distinguishes the analysis of evil."[15] For Simone Weil, this inverted dichotomy is easily explained: "Imaginary evil is romantic and varied; real evil is gloomy, monotonous, barren, boring. Imaginary good is boring; real good is always new, marvelous, intoxicating."[16] Freely disagree with Weil here, but honesty requires us to concede that—Jane Austen's Anne Elliot to the contrary—Sister Mariella's summons has gone in the main unfulfilled, though not for lack of trying.

As her misanthropic husband takes a mistress, the novel's protagonist Vera roots herself in bulls—not taunting the brutal beauties of Hemingway's matadors but raising prize animals and serving as "president of the Red Poll Breeder's Association of the Atlantic Seaboard States."[17] *The Malefactors* dramatizes the vows of marriage as they're threshed and tested on the extreme rock-bottom floor of infidelity; its hard-won wisdom concerning the art of male-female relations offers a heap of wisdom for anyone.

In *How to Read a Novel*, Gordon cites Aristotle, contending that all great narrative art falls into two parts: complication and resolution: "The Resolution is always embedded in the Complication from the very start."[18] *The Malefactor*'s complication commences on page one. Waking late, Vera's husband, Tom, rises on the day of the *fête* to find her leading the tame prize bull. At once we behold one of the novel's controlling symbols (the Red Poll), and we grasp their marital *de facto* separation as he

---

15. Cited in Joshua Hren, "The Catholic Writer of the Future," *Dappled Things*, June 2022, https://www.dappledthings.org/reviews/the-catholic -writer-of-the-future-a-review-of-many-colored-fleece.

16. Simone Weil, "Morality and Literature," in *On Science, Necessity, and the Love of God* (Oxford: Oxford University Press), 160–166.

17. Gordon, *The Malefactors*, 10.

18. Caroline Gordon, *How to Read a Novel* (Providence, RI: Cluny, 2019), 26.

wearyingly resists each of her requests with the same palpable indifference.

Tom wants to avoid a visit to his aunt's sickroom, where Cat Pollard (aka "Dorothy Day") is looking human fragility in the face. He wants someone else to pick up Vera's cousin Cynthia from the train station, but when he grudgingly fulfills his wife's request, things get complicated quickly. Tom and Cynthia's interactions are charged with indirect but evident erotic tension. On the ride home, Cynthia speaks glibly of her strained marriage, and Tom emerges as a potential Paulo to this Dantean "Francesca"—*figura* of forbidden love in the circle of the lustful.

Tom, like many another poet, is a difficult man to love, a fact that elevates Vera in the reader's troubled heart; still, although it is hard to witness his habitual solipsism, Gordon renders his own agonies with soft touches that solicit concern for his soul rather than condemnation. His mentor Horne Watts committed suicide by leaping from a transatlantic ship. This abdication into the abyss oppresses Tom throughout the novel. Seeing Cynthia sitting on a bench in "the shadow of a tree trunk," he wonders, as "she set her cup down and leaned father backward . . . Did she know that her bench stood on the lip of a chasm?"[19] Sometimes he's tempted to follow the man to whom he remains in debt. Tom never had a proper raising; his tormented father, a gambler who frequented whorehouses, frequently ghosts the novel: "He could not ever remember looking his father in the face without feeling the necessity to look away. . . . It was not because his father had looked unkind or arrogant that he had found it necessary to avert his gaze from his face, but because he looked unhappy," and, for children, "unhappiness is the cardinal sin."[20]

"The past is never dead. It's not even past," wrote William Faulkner in *Requiem for a Nun*.[21] Gordon's Faulkner-haunted novel

19. Gordon, *The Malefactors*, 72.

20. Gordon, 51.

21. William Faulkner, *Requiem for a Nun* (New York: Vintage, 2012), 73.

plants this germ in unexpected places and watches what happens when past blooms through the cracks of the present-tense action. As Gordon explained to a friend, three dead men (the poet Horne Watts, as well as the fathers of Tom and Vera) "unfold chronologically, counterclockwise to the main action."[22] In "Nature and Grace in Caroline Gordon," Louise Cowan addresses Gordon's purposive disruption of linear narrative: "Though the surface of her novels . . . moves toward destruction and despair, the current in their depths moves in a strongly different direction."[23] Gordon's muse is a sort of Christian Janus who cranes our necks backward to keep us in awe and ache over our complex inheritance: our actions and decisions, if not governed by a deterministic fate, are nonetheless always fraught with our forebears' successes and failures.

Tom's early poetic achievements won him laurels and editorships, but he cannot conscientiously ride on the coattails of these youthful victories. In shame, he has "fallen into the habit of deceiving [Vera]."[24] Although he has written only a handful of pages of middling poetry in many years, each day he asserts that "I've got some things to do," and, shutting himself into his office, he locks the door. The lock is a safeguard against shame; once, a servant entered the room to find the poet asleep on the sofa instead of communing at the altar of the Muse.

And so it is no surprise when Cynthia, houseguest at Blencker's Bridge, appears in Tom's office "in a white dress," bearing a manila folder filled with poetry. Cognizant of the dried-up irrigation ditch that separates him from his wife, she seizes upon his declaration of poetic impotence, indicating how eager she is to have him admire her poems and then trading his confession

22. Christine Flanagan, ed., *The Letters of Flannery O'Connor and Caroline Gordon* (Athens, GA: University of Georgia Press, 2018), 91.

23. Louise Cowan, "Nature and Grace in Caroline Gordon," *Critique: Studies in Contemporary Fiction* 1, no. 1 (1956): 13.

24. Gordon, *The Malefactors*, 143.

for a volatile confidence. Although Tom knew that Vera's father committed suicide, Cynthia takes pleasure in telling him more, reveling in a family secret locked up in the attic—in the Claiborne attic just above them.

Tom and Cynthia ascend into the attic, and just before they open the aluminum container concealing the forbidden knowledge, Cynthia starts pressing closer to him, whispering his name. He raises his head to find his wife as witness to their proximate infidelities. Vera lies, averting "her eyes from his while she contrived the first lie she had ever told him."[25] It is obvious that Cynthia was keen to Vera's secret. In this, the novel's fall, it is obvious that Vera's first falsehood is in part a consequence of Cynthia's cruelty and of her husband's own flirtations with misspent intimacies.

The affair between Tom and Cynthia accelerates, as they consummate their predictable passions. She takes up an apartment in New York City, and he assumes an editorial position at *Parade*, a newly launched literary magazine. As Anne M. Boyle writes in *Strange and Lurid Bloom: A Study of the Fiction of Caroline Gordon*, the author "turns her attention to the salvation of the frustrated . . . intellectual" who needs to recover his manhood.[26] Tom's adultery is a cheap assertion of virility, whereas his assumption of an editorial position requires daily work. Soon thereafter it "occurred to him that he had spent half his life avoiding offices."[27] The discipline that his duties demand reorients his restless soul, and, unexpectedly, he experiences "stirrings of his imagination" for the first time in years.[28]

The last third of the novel is leavened with ironies and reversals. Tom does not end up in a bohemian hovel; instead, his absent friends offer him (and perhaps implicitly Cynthia) their

25. Gordon, 166.
26. Boyle, *Strange and Lurid Bloom*, 168.
27. Gordon, *The Malefactors*, 220.
28. Gordon, 220.

ornate apartment, a habitation so gaudy that, as a drunken guest once admits, "*You*—in this apartment! Several people told me about it, but I had to see it to believe it."[29] The inebriated Molly does more than mock the dissonance between Tom's literary pretentions and this exorbitant locale. Pulling her into a dark room, he finds he prefers the lightlessness, which as though conceals "from the world at large . . . some poverty."[30] Gordon's articulation of the paradox is perfect: the ornamentation and lavishness of his borrowed apartment, when revealed, expose Tom's deepest impoverishment. He has gained the whole world in exchange for a starving soul.

Tom retreats into that familiar, shallow solipsism and peddles the platitude that "people our age often discover that their first marriages were a mistake," but his protest is no match for Cynthia's sunken countenance, which he is forced to confront once Molly and the party guests exit.[31] "There was an expression on her face that he had never seen before," he muses, "as if somebody you had never seen or heard of were suddenly standing at the window of a house you had supposed unoccupied."[32] Gordon takes us into yet another room of meaning, down another one of these crooked corridors with which their borrowed home is pregnant. Beyond the pleasantries of poetry, beyond the pressings of the flesh, he does not know Cynthia at all, does not realize that she is using him for his reputation and influence, as a temporary residence from which to launch her writing career. For his part, Tom denies his love of Vera with the devastating admission that "I'm not in love with any woman," the indirect confession that he cares only for himself.[33] He is visited by a fierce desire to be covered in darkness.

29. Gordon, 281.
30. Gordon, 282.
31. Gordon, 282.
32. Gordon, 284.
33. Gordon, 286.

Into the lightlessness he has courted with such passion comes a remarkable divine intrusion, sending seeds of conversion into his consciousness—foreign words whose source momentarily eludes him: *While all things were in quiet silence and night was in the midst of her course.* The words are from the Word, from Wisdom. In the biblical book, this scene of night silence is succeeded by the following: "Thy almighty word leapt down from heaven from thy royal throne as a fierce conqueror into the midst of the land of destruction" (18:4–5 Douay-Rheims). These words wrestle with his wasteland soul until, though still harsh, he has heart enough to profess his awfulness and Vera's goodness. The scene's pitch could break glass, and at last Tom's most obfuscating window, dirtied by impossible smudges, shatters. Although he is unable to tell Cynthia what she is, if she is "not a woman," when his lover asks him what *he* is ("And you? What are *you*?"), he can finally look inside and find the right words: "A son of a bitch. That's what I am. A son of a bitch."[34] And with that he leaves the room.

There is something in this scene of the Greek tragedy's "reversal" that Aristotle describes in his *Poetics*. In *How to Read a Novel*, Gordon explains that the reversal is caused "by an incident: something which, happening suddenly, crystalizes the action and hurries it toward Resolution."[35] Although "there is nothing illogical about it" (and there is nothing illogical in this reversal of *The Malefactors*), "it has in it all the elements of surprise which make a plot . . . work."[36] Tom's confession seemed permanently deferred; we should not have been surprised had he withheld it even until the curtains closed on the novel's last page. However, we have been waiting, *hoping* that he could name his sin.

Denigrating himself in front of his temporary muse is a major gain, but his name-calling remains vague—it does not reach the precision that real conversion requires. The substantive

---

34. Gordon, 286.

35. Gordon, *How to Read a Novel*, 32.

36. Gordon, 33.

turning starts when Tom arrives at the outskirts of "Mary Farm," where his wife has gone to "tend pigs"—with all the abandon of an ascetic. Gordon reintroduces one of the novel's controlling symbols: on the literal level, we find that Vera has given her "prize bull" to the Catholic Worker farm.[37] But, as Cheney explains, "he also signifies the brass bull, in which St. Eustice and his family were burned to death."[38] The animal, which the novel breeds us to read as affiliated with martyrdom, moves from the source of Vera's pride to alms for the poor. But this symbol is only an allegorical predecessor of the radical conversions that follow in its stead.

If Vera is manifestly regenerate, Gordon lets Tom be Tom. He moves from the precipice of sorrow to resentful paranoia. If Vera decides not to get a divorce, he concludes, her fidelity could only have an ugly motive: maybe she's plotting to adopt a child, and "the authorities don't like broken homes, as we laughingly call them."[39] She could marry again, in a few months, he mocks. She should just get a divorce. His words are refined instruments of torture: "Spend the rest of your life working in an orphan asylum," he says, "or an insane asylum, if that suits you better. . . . Have a religious conversion!" "I think maybe I have had it!" she shouts back.[40] The double entendre is just right: yes, yes, she has had it with Tom's antics, and, yes, yes, she has had that conversion. It is only left for him to follow. In the words of the novel's epigraph, taken from Jacques Maritain, "It is for Adam to interpret the voices that Eve hears" (that this passage had a profound personal resonance for Gordon is evident in that the line is etched on her tombstone).[41]

But between Tom's tantrums and predictable self-pity, a run-in with Cat Pollard pierces his predictable, defeatist self-pity.

37. Gordon, *The Malefactors*, 268.

38. Cheney, "Caroline Gordon's 'The Malefactors'," 366.

39. Gordon, *The Malefactors*, 328.

40. Gordon, 328.

41. Gordon, 1.

He hastens to Mary Farm, where "he could sleep in the hay if there was no bed. He could be sitting there on the bench with the other bums when she came down in the morning."[42] The allusion to Christ's parable of the prodigal is plain. It works on the reader both literally and allusively—efficaciously, on both levels—because Gordon has established the agrarian backdrop from page one. Here is a brushstroke of Bethlehem. Gordon mixes the action of grace into the dried-out palette of her own marriage, marking the horizon with the color of hope that he could, like Christ, be born in the hay. He could, we know, be born again into a second sight, if he is already willing to see himself a bum.

In addition to being a saving mentor, Gordon was a Catholic novelist of considerable talent. She appears on the scene like a "Lost Generation" matador with an impressive *muleta*—that stick-hung cloth bullfighters bring out for the last third of the match. Her red cloth is rich with the threads of so many masters: Faulkner and Flaubert, James Joyce and Henry James. In his *Commonweal* review of *The Malefactors*, Fr. John W. Simons finds in Gordon "a novelist who had not only avoided with her usual consistency the *clichés* of her craft but had come closer"[43] than any other Catholic writer to "encompassing the elusive miracle" of rendering conversion in an artistically arresting way without cheapening either nature or grace. Like Flannery, we have much to learn from her, not least the graceful way by which she slouches the lost creature back to Bethlehem to be born.

(Note: Portions of this essay previously appeared in *America*, "Caroline Gordon, the Catholic novelist we lost and found," April 21, 2001, https://www.americamagazine.org/arts-culture/2021/04/01/ caroline-gordon-malefactors-catholic-novelist-240356.)

42. Gordon, 338.

43. John W. Simons, "A Cunning and Curious Dramatization," *Commonweal* 64, no. 2 (April 13, 1956): 54–56, cited in Cheney, "Caroline Gordon's 'The Malefactors'," 369.

RECOMMENDED READING

Christine Flanagan, ed. *The Letters of Flannery O'Connor and Caroline Gordon*.

Caroline Gordon. *The Malefactors*.

_____. *How to Read a Novel*.

_____. *The House of Fiction*.

_____. *The Collected Stories of Caroline Gordon*.

_____. *The Strange Children*.

Joshua Hren is founder of Wiseblood Books and co-founder of the Master of Fine Arts in Creative Writing at the University of St. Thomas, Houston. Joshua has written seven books, including the novel *Infinite Regress* and the theological-aesthetical manifesto *Contemplative Realism*.

Rumer Godden:
Listening with the Inner Ear

Katy Carl

"I have an inner ear, 'voices' that, if I listen to them, save me from going wrong; if I listen I do right and, in fact, as I listen, an awareness comes of something in myself larger than myself, a feeling of being allied, that I am guided."—Rumer Godden, *A House with Four Rooms*[1]

INTRODUCTION

Among acknowledged Catholic writers of the twentieth century, Rumer Godden (1907–1998) stands with those who are best beloved for what may be their least "literary" works. One of Godden's gifts was to bridge the gap between "popular" and "literary" writing: her works are richly embroidered, vividly colored, at times meandering, and yet capable of reaching unsuspected depths, despite what one critic saw as "naïve faults of construction."[2] Godden's contribution to the good books of

---

1. Rumer Godden, *A House with Four Rooms* (New York: William Morrow, 1989), 44.

2. Godden, on being told by her agent Spencer Curtis Brown that her sister's fiction contained "naïve faults of construction," said that she had not perceived these faults, only to be told in return that her own fiction was prone to them as well. The episode is related in Anne Chisholm, *Rumer Godden: A Storyteller's Life* (London: Macmillan, 1998), 194.

the twentieth century extends well beyond her contribution to explicitly Catholic-themed literature. Her work remains beloved in two worlds, taking up Catholic themes both before and after her conversion to the Church.

Godden's fascination with Catholicism and with religious belief and practice in general long predated her formal—and unlikely—conversion to the faith. Of her return to Christianity, Godden writes in *A House with Four Rooms* that over the course of several years without a spiritual home in young adulthood, she slowly grew into a feeling that she "must have something . . . far beyond myself to hold on to."[3] Though her mostly nonpracticing Anglican family never fully understood her choice, Godden knew her soul had found its home in Catholicism.

Godden's innate feel for reverence first bloomed during her childhood as the daughter of well-to-do British businesspeople living in India, a childhood that she describes in *A Time to Dance, No Time to Weep* as involving "a mingling of religions"[4] among the people she knew. Her family worked with a Catholic ayah (nanny or *au pair*), Muslim and Buddhist household staff, and outdoor helpers from both Brahmin and Dalit backgrounds. This gave the child Rumer a sense of the potential for harmonious cooperation among believers from differing traditions. Her father, Arthur, reinforced this lesson, both positively through his own respect for the diverse people with whom he dealt in business and at home, and once through a severe reprimand when young Rumer taunted a Hindu gardener by using one of his tradition's words for the divine disrespectfully. Arthur insisted on an apology from Rumer, who felt ashamed of her misstep—especially as, by her

3. Godden, *A House with Four Rooms*, 70.

4. Rumer Godden, *A Time to Dance, No Time to Weep* (New York: William Morrow, 1987), 2.

own admission, she was not then fully aware that religions had "edges" or boundaries between them. Disrespect to one form of belief became, for her, synonymous with disrespect toward all.

Perhaps this helps to explain why Godden's adolescent run-in with religious sisters tended to skew her early beliefs toward a vague, spiritually tinged agnosticism. As a young writer, she intended her breakthrough novel *Black Narcissus* as an "attack" or act of revenge against a group of cruel nuns who briefly had the charge of the Godden sisters' education in their adolescent years. (The nuns in the novel may be read as either Catholic or High Anglican; this is never made fully clear.) Seeing that the girls were half-foreign in speech and behavior because of their childhood in India, these English nuns indulged themselves in snobbish prejudice against and scapegoating of the newcomers. Rumer and her older sister, Jon, endured public shamings and senseless punishments over truly minor infractions, in an atmosphere that contained no sign of the reverence for creation and for human dignity that the girls had been so comprehensively taught to regard as the sign of holiness. The height of the episode came when the girls' mother, hoping to spare her daughters awkwardness, took advantage of a technical permission to release them from chapel attendance—a move that only inflamed the nuns' spite against the Goddens and redoubled their hostilities. Not long afterward, their mother became aware of how her daughters were being treated and pulled them out of the convent school.

Throughout that time, young Rumer saw in the nuns' behavior the precise opposite of their purported beliefs and, in her own mind, struck back harshly against their hypocrisy and empty pharisaism. Yet while *Black Narcissus* will still bear this reading, Godden's innate artistry also guided her better than she knew at the time. Though it concerns the deconstruction of some characters' immature faith, the novel can equally well be read as a clear-eyed tragic study of what happens to the consecrated life when its inner heart of devotion to Christ goes cold. Godden's biographer Anne Chisholm also reads the novel as a working analogy for the failure of British rule in India, a description that could fit many of Godden's other works.

In her memoir *A House with Four Rooms*, Godden tells how her heart was drawn gradually back, first toward the Anglicanism of the beloved aunts in whose care she had once spent eighteen months and then, unexpectedly for her, toward Catholicism. In 1957, she entered the Church, and the friendship she soon afterward developed with the nuns of Stanbrook Abbey would prove definitive both for her spiritual life and for her later career.

Godden treats the first overtures of her adult conversion with characteristic humor. In one memorable episode, her children end up not at the Easter church service she sent them to but instead with their caregiver at the seaside. Yet in Godden's character, as biographer Anne Chisholm notices, reverence and good humor were twin sisters. Of the consecrated characters who are still some of her most beloved and of their real-life counterparts, Godden writes that their stories are intrinsically "dramatic" because they live "the greatest love story in the world."[5] Godden's attitude of reverence and respect toward people of all faiths and toward whatever is legitimately good in their spiritual values resonates with the teaching of Vatican II's constitution *Lumen Gentium* on the protoevangelical character of the human religious impulse. At the same time, Godden appreciated the clarity of a distinctively Catholic approach to life, which she explained in pithy form: "You'll always be forgiven, but you must know the rules."[6]

A LIFE IN LITERATURE

"In the worst times, if we can manage to get through to each other, even, it will keep something alive that is vital to us and I think too vital to the world. Naturally I don't mean our work

5. Chisholm, *Rumer Godden*, 262.
6. Chisholm, 251.

is vital to the world but that the spirit of which we have a patch is vital." —Rumer Godden, August 1939 letter to her sister Jon[7]

Like many successful women writers, Godden lived a life of fluent productivity that was confluent with her family and community life. Not only did she turn out, at a rapid pace, a constant supply of new and well-crafted novels, short fiction, poetry, essays, literary journalism, and memoirs—all in the face of considerable challenges on personal, professional, and societal levels—but at the same time, she also gave generously of her time to building culture within and through relationships. At different seasons of her life she worked as a dance instructor, a home educator, a wartime volunteer, a scriptwriter and consultant for films based on her own books, a homesteader (this phase did not last long), and a teacher of poetry to schoolchildren.

Never very skilled as a housekeeper—she recounts her fumbling through domestic work and her complicated working relationships with many household helpers humorously in *A House with Four Rooms*[8]—still, Godden loved growing food and flowers in her garden, working with animals, and spending time with her own children and those of her many friends. Though conventional social gatherings in public places and British-style "clubs" made her anxious and shy, Godden enjoyed visiting friends' homes and hosting them in hers.

As a young woman, Godden weathered a variety of losses and reversals that might have ended the work of a writer less resilient or less sure of her direction. When their two daughters were young, Godden's first husband ran up debts that devoured her earnings from *Black Narcissus* and cost him the trust of both his employers and his wife. He then went into the army to serve

---

7. Chisholm, 90.

8. A delightful coincidence is that on Godden's return to the English country-side after sojourns in London and Kolkata, she lived for a time in the same house that had once been inhabited by fellow Catholic novelist Sheila Kaye-Smith. She also spent time living in Lamb House, famously the last residence of Henry James.

in World War II. Afterward, the pair made heartfelt, drawn-out attempts at reconciliation—which, despite good intentions on both sides, failed. It became clear that they had married under duress, because of Godden's first pregnancy, and in a state of serious immaturity on both sides. After her conversion, Godden reported a feeling of regret that she had ever been able to take the reality of the marriage bond so lightly.

With very few resources, and unable to go back to England because of the ongoing war, Godden moved with her girls to Kashmir, where they rented first a suburban house and then a small cottage in the mountains called Dove House. They lived there until an extraordinary and still unresolved incident in which Godden, her daughters, and a guest found crushed glass and intoxicating substances in their food, making them temporarily but seriously ill. In the resulting tangle of legal proceedings, Godden and her daughters left Dove House to take refuge—first in her sister's house in Kolkata and then in England, where Godden's parents still lived. Here as in India, Godden continued to move house frequently, always with the sense that the fresh start would reduce her expenses and resolve domestic complications.

After her first marriage ended, Godden was courted by a friend who had fallen in love with her, James Haynes-Dixon. She grew to have a great affection for him, yet for years she resisted marrying him. Looking back on that time, Godden wrote of how she wanted to preserve her hard-won stability of life and the gifts of their easy companionship, but it seems possible she may have also feared another radical betrayal of her trust. Eventually, James won Rumer over by his consistent loyalty, his practical kindness to herself and her children, and his support of her writing. They married in 1949 just as Rumer was preparing to visit India for the filming of her novel *The River* with director Jean Renoir. By this time both James and Rumer had been wounded by life and set in their habits, so it took work to adapt to each other and to the demands of their vocation.

Yet Godden, never one to back down from a challenge, took a long view of their relationship's inevitable tensions: "No one will ever know what he is to me," she wrote to her sister in 1950, "and for that I have to accept the rest. Remember, too, he pours out his all for me and I am very difficult as you know."[9] As the season of adjustment passed, the pair entered "calmer waters." Godden's letters draw a picture of a partnership that was mutually tender and supportive and, on James' side, perhaps a shade too protective—to the extent that he once ended up in a fistfight with her literary agent over questions of her best interest.

Throughout all these changes and preoccupations, Godden never lapsed in her responsibility to her work as a writer. With rare exceptions, her mornings and sometimes also her evenings belonged consistently to the development and production of her books. Often she would rise before dawn, sometimes as early as 4:30 a.m., to write before her children awoke. She wrote even while traveling, through illnesses, and despite a host of practical problems. For Godden, this self-disciplined life was both an economic necessity and an artistic duty. By the revenue it brought in and the regularity of the habits it required, her writing helped to give her family a much-desired sense of stability.

This set of stable dispositions may also have led to another rare achievement Godden managed: writing works of equal quality for both children and adults, enjoyable across age lines in both directions. It is not always easy to tell, simply from the reading experience, which of Godden's works are aimed at children and which at adults. Both her children's and adults' novels succeed at depicting children as full human beings whose difficulty articulating their experience sharpens rather than dulls the intensity of that experience. *An Episode of Sparrows*, recently re-released in a New York Review of Books children's edition, still reads more like a novel about children for adults rather than

9. Chisholm, 243.

for children expressly, though it could be handed to a bright ten-year-old with no qualms. *The Greengage Summer*, also sometimes listed as one of Godden's "children's" novels, deals precisely with childhood's last days, early adolescence, and the long, slow passage into an adult understanding of life. So does *The River*, one of her most autobiographical works. Long before "young adult" or "YA" literature was a live category in publishing, Godden recognized that readers of all ages deserve to be written for in ways that acknowledge their reason, their dignity, and their need for literary art that corresponds in a vibrant way to reality.

Godden was drawn to education and the arts both as a matter of economic necessity and of God-given talent. Biographer Anne Chisholm brings across the contrast between Rumer and her slightly older sister, Jon, who was also a novelist, though her work was of a "cooler" and "darker,"[10] more obscure and less popular, tone than Rumer's: Jon believed that Rumer wrote too fast, revised too little, and spread herself too thin to achieve all she should have been capable of on the page. Rumer believed that Jon held back too much, worked too slowly, and sometimes lacked the courage of her artistic convictions. Yet there was no antipathy between the sisters in all this. No one else thought more highly of, or relied more heavily on, Jon's opinions on the art of fiction. Rumer also gently yet frequently prodded Jon to write more often and more boldly. The two remained in lively correspondence, sharing practical help, mutual encouragement, family news, and trenchant notes on craft, until Jon's death in 1984. Though the pair also had two younger sisters, with whom they stayed closely and supportively in touch, it was Jon, the main companion of her childhood, who seemed to be most psychologically and intellectually important to Rumer. Characters based more or less entirely on Jon appear in many of Rumer's fictions.

10. Chisholm, 203.

CATHOLIC NOVELIST, SELECTIVE REALIST?

In Catholic circles today, Godden's name is nearly synonymous with her meandering, winsome, and in places sentimental yarn of religious life, *In This House of Brede*, which in its most recent edition from Cluny Media runs near four hundred pages. This work is well worth loving for its beauty of prose, closeness of observation, and gentle, humane, and persistent insight into the inalienable goodness of wounded human nature. Yet its scale of values seems to have been drawn at a greater remove from common experience than is the case in most of Godden's work. Undeniably, the book has moved and continues to move thousands of readers. Many early fans wrote effusively to Godden to tell her of graces and joys it brought them.

Yet, just as undeniably, the shadow of sin at the abbey of Brede is not wholly absent but is largely effaced. Godden herself spoke of the difficulties of working "conflict and drama" believably into a reverent novel of authentically peaceful contemplative life. The result, in certain passages, shades beyond impressionism into blurriness. Can *In This House of Brede*, this so much beloved novel, justly be brought up as evidence that—as many Catholic writers of the twentieth and twenty-first centuries have feared—a writer's increase in devotion (or in sympathetic attention to devout characters) must also mean a decrease in artistic quality?

Godden's other novels of religious life can serve to help us reach an answer.[11] In these novels, the devoted reader is likelier to find sharper and clearer pictures of reality, ones that more readily meet the criteria Raïssa Maritain laid out for Catholic literature:

---

11. It is only fair to note that my reading of these works differs from Godden's own. In *A House with Four Rooms*, she writes that, having established friendships with real nuns after her conversion, she "blushed" (239) for the memory of *Black Narcissus* and considered *In This House of Brede* to be much the more realist treatment of the two. It may be more realist about how grace can transfigure and elevate human nature, while *Black Narcissus* is more realist about the tendency of human nature to bend away from the good when its relationship to grace is attenuated—which can happen even in consecrated life.

"No timidity. No pharisaism. No ignorance. No prudishness. No Manicheism."[12]

These five desiderata find their fulfillment, under different modes, in Godden's breakout novel *Black Narcissus* and in her late-career revisitation of religious community *Five for Sorrow, Ten for Joy*. While other structural defects plague the latter—mainly errors of pacing, unusual in a dramatist of Godden's keenness—its heart for lost and broken souls beats with the very compassion of Christ. Though it has received only passing mention in recent Catholic media, *Five for Sorrow, Ten for Joy* deserves wider and closer reading in Catholic circles, as it examines without sentimentality both the ruinous harm done by sexual and emotional abuse—especially of the very young—and the healing potential of devotion to Mary, whose capacity to lead souls closer to Christ's love Godden plainly and powerfully makes clear through the story's course. Key to the realism of *Five for Sorrow, Ten for Joy* is its use of a (metaphorical) chiaroscuro: not every soul is saved within the novel's necessarily closed horizon, not every harm it depicts can be undone, but its sources and refractions of light shine forth all the stronger for the depth of the evils they must resist.

Likewise, *Black Narcissus* is, for Catholic readers, a largely undiscovered gem, both as an artistic triumph of contrasts and as a close examination of themes that feel even fresher today than at the time Godden released the novel. First published in 1939, *Black Narcissus* centers around a fictional community of Western nuns who, in their attempts to make a new foundation of their order in the Himalayas, run across startling obstacles from within and without. Not only are the sisters unprepared for the challenges of interfaith and cross-class communication that their new environment demands, but they are thwarted by their naïveté about human nature. This naïveté leaves them blind to the refusals of grace, attachments to the world, and attractions

---

12. Jacques Maritain, ed., *The Journal of Raïssa Maritain* (Providence, RI: Cluny, 2020), 70.

of the body and soul lurking within themselves. The novel's dialogic imagination explores how devotion can fail as, one by one, the sisters break out or break down in ways that surprise both themselves and the reader.

In its treatment of how far inculturation of Christian faith in Asian societies is possible, *Black Narcissus* has surprising resonance with Shūsaku Endō's classic Catholic novel *Silence*. The line delivered by the wise Sister Phillipa—"I think there are only two ways to live in this place . . . either ignore it completely or give yourself up to it"[13]—recalls the apostate missionary Ferreira's claim in *Silence* that Christianity in Eastern countries is a non-native plant, an invasive species that cannot grow in the "swamp"[14] soil of Japan, which, however fertile, prefers native flora. Interestingly, though both Godden's other "India novels" and Endō's *The Samurai* suggest possible forms of resolution to this and similar seeming contradictions between faith and culture, such potentialities for reconciliation remain all but absent from both *Silence* and *Black Narcissus*. Hints are given in Mr. Dean's description of the open-air cloister chapel he would like to build for the sisters, though the novel quickly dismisses the possibility of the sisters' accepting such a compromise. *Black Narcissus* also only hints at the potential for scapegoating violence that, in *Silence*, is fully realized.

Like Endō, Godden is honoring, through art, the irreducibility of real divergences in Western and Eastern systems of thought and belief. Both novelists are alert to the dangers, up to and including loss of souls, caused by patronizing attitudes toward indigenous systems. Such oversimplification, they both perceive, can be rooted in fearful refusal to fully understand differing beliefs rather than work toward a mutual understanding that trusts in the power of truth. *Black Narcissus* also successfully explores the

13. Rumer Godden, *Black Narcissus* (London: Albatross, 1947), 164.

14. Shūsaku Endō, *Silence*, trans. William Johnston (Marlboro, NJ: Taplinger, 1969), 147.

ways in which devotion to even the deepest truth can go wrong when human efforts clash with both grace and nature. Though her human heart brought wounds to the endeavor, the artist in Godden also brought remarkable perceptivity and insight, so that her novel continues to serve as a chilling and relevant cautionary tale.

Throughout her career, Godden depicted characters with both European and Asian, both Western and Eastern, characteristics and heritages. She particularly sought out those figures who could somehow reconcile in themselves the diversity of influences that had come to bear on her own childhood and formation. Working with these figures, Godden deepens perennial, universal themes: the passage from innocence into experience; the redemptive powers of faith and of community; the transformative powers and inherent risks of human sexuality; the simplicity and purity of the natural world versus the complications and tumults of human society; tension and confluence between divergent cultures and religions; and relationships between parents and children and across barriers of race, class, and gender. Though including a diverse range of characters, Godden never drew caricatures. Her novels give us real people with genuine traits, quirks, and individualities—one almost wants to say *souls*.

Godden's fictions of belief, rather than being mired in doubt over the truth claims of religion and the credibility of sometimes compromised temporal authority, are instead characterized by wonder and reverence toward almost any legitimate form the human religious impulse can take. At the same time, Godden is both unsurprised and undaunted by human fallibilities and infidelities. Her vision encompassed people as she found them. Her narrators often share her own uncommon powers for appreciating human goodness wherever it is found, for holding in sight both the horror of wrongdoing and a gentle compassion for those who have done wrong.

CONCLUSION

Reading Godden's work in any genre gives the feeling of watching a skilled fabric artist run material through her fingers, smoothly using various tools to produce elaborate, highly ordered new structures. The fabrics of Godden's choice are the English language and her own sense of closely observed reality. With these she produces vibrant tapestries that echo the deceptive simplicities and unexpected profundities of the natural and spiritual beauties that delighted her. The resulting work produces the sense of enchantment that is the proper effect of *poiesis*.

RECOMMENDED READING

Fiction

Rumer Godden. *Black Narcissus.*
————. *A Candle for St. Jude.*
————. *The Dark Horse.*
————. *Five for Sorrow, Ten for Joy.*
————. *In This House of Brede.*

Memoir

Rumer Godden. *A House with Four Rooms.*
————. *A Time to Dance, No Time to Weep.*

Other

Anne Chisholm. *Rumer Godden: A Storyteller's Life.*
Hassel Simpson. *Rumer Godden* (Twayne's English Authors Series).
The Rumer Godden Literary Trust. rumergodden.com

Katy Carl is editor-in-chief of *Dappled Things* magazine, a partner of the Ars Vivendi Initiative through the Collegium Institute. She is author of *As Earth Without Water*, a novel; *Fragile Objects*, a collection of short stories; and *Praying the Great O Antiphons*, a book of meditations. She is a senior affiliate fellow of the Program for Research on Religion and Urban Civil Society, and she lives in the Houston area with her husband and their family.

Alice Thomas Ellis:
Bohemian Traditionalist

Bonnie Lander Johnson

Anna Margaret Haycraft (1932–2005), known to her readers as Alice Thomas Ellis, was a journalist, novelist, painter, cookery book writer, fiction editor, mother of seven, and a member of the Camden literary milieu. With her husband she ran the Duckworth Press, for many years housed in a building at the end of the road on which they lived. In the 1980s and '90s she was considered one of Britain's finest novelists; now she is largely remembered only in Catholic circles, and not for her fiction but for her controversial defenses of the preconciliar Church and her open criticism of Derek Worlock, Archbishop of Liverpool, positions that have earned her the label of iconoclast and reactionary.

Ellis turned rather late to writing. Her first novel, *The Sin Eater* (1977), centers around a female character loosely based on Ellis herself, who voices criticisms of the postconciliar Church. Ellis wrote the novel under her pseudonym because she was already well known in the publishing world. When her identity was discovered, Ellis instead embraced the role of controversial Catholic. *The Sin Eater* is uneven stylistically and narratively, perhaps constrained by Ellis' desire to articulate her own opinions in fictional form. For a short while after its publication, Ellis claimed she would not write another novel. Then her nineteen-year-old son Joshua died, and in her bereavement she turned again to writing. *The Birds of the Air* (1980) is a dark comedy in which a bereaved mother longs to follow her child into death. The novel is an alarming and highly successful piece of narrative artistry that established Ellis as one of the best British voices of the late twentieth century. She went on to write three more novels, all of which deployed her characteristic short-form, witty dialogue, and unnerving, almost supernatural, plots: *The 27th Kingdom* (1982), *The Other Side of the Fire* (1983), and *Unexplained Laughter* (1985). She then began three novels that formed *The Summerhouse Trilogy*, perhaps her greatest work of fiction: *The Clothes in the Wardrobe* (1987), *The Skeleton in the Cupboard* (1988), and *The Fly in the Ointment* (1990). Four more novels followed in the 1990s: *The Inn at the Edge of the World* (1990), *Pillars of Gold* (1992), *Fairy Tale* (1996), and *Hotel Lucifer* (1999). She also wrote cookery books, nonfiction collaborations with the psychologist Tom Pitt-Aikens, and autobiographical accounts such as *A Welsh Childhood* (1990).

In London, Ellis is perhaps remembered most for her central role in the Camden literary coterie. Her large and eccentric Gloucester Terrace household was well known for its conflation of home life, writing, painting, and publishing; in this convergence of activity, Ellis' home has been compared to the Bloomsbury group. But Ellis was not Virginia Woolf. Although, like many good Catholics, she preferred the company of artists and inebriates to that of saints or aristocrats, Ellis was no political progressive but a defender of ancient moral codes disappearing with terrifying rapidity from the nation's conscience, especially in the second half of the twentieth century. Nor was Ellis particularly interested in the personal satisfactions or creative triumphs of art; painting and writing were simply ways to spend the time allotted to her. One of the century's most sought-after fiction editors, she was only in publishing because it was her husband's calling.

She regularly claimed that had her husband been a tailor she would have sewn his buttons. Ellis' indifference to any careerist identification with the numerous talents she commanded left one interviewer exasperated: "You're not a novelist, not a journalist, not an artist and not a cook. So what are you?" "A Catholic," she answered without a second's thought.

The one insistent atmosphere at the heart of everything Ellis wrote was the home. Whether speaking from her "Home Life" column in *The Spectator* or through the voice of one of her numerous fictional female characters, Ellis demands that her readers take their place beside her in a household where for most of the twentieth century the kitchen table bore the weight of endless manuscripts, canvases, and cats and provided food and conversation for the constant traffic of children, friends, neighbors, religious, and authors seeking publication.

For Ellis, all work, all writing, emerged from the intimacy of the domestic world for which she was loved and renowned; she put the Catholic experience of home and the friendships of women center stage within the public and masculine world of English literature and letters. And yet she was no feminist. On the contrary, she frequently asserted that the many joys and blessings in her life, or any claims she could make to what is now understood as female "emancipation" or "freedom," were given to her by the traditions and doctrines of the Catholic Church and most definitely *not* by feminism. "I believe that if forced to choose with whom I would prefer to spend a few hours, I would opt for football hooligans rather than face the malignant ferocity of a roomful of would-be lady priests and discontented nuns."[1]

Every traditional Catholic feels in their blood a pull toward the Church's two great vocations, the religious orders and family life. Ellis knew both firsthand. She was a happy preconciliar postulant in Liverpool until a spinal injury meant she had to leave her

1. Alice Thomas Ellis, *God Has Not Changed* (London: Burns & Oates, 2004), 122.

order. Subsequently, she married Colin Haycraft and settled into the London literary world. In their different but complementary ways, conventual life and family life place the household at the center of daily existence. Not the fantastical middle-class household of the nineteenth and early twentieth centuries, with its angel at the hearth and cozy material perfection, but a working household in which all members labor, eat, talk, and pray. Ellis' weekly column for *The Spectator* chronicled with superb irony the endless demands on the "housewife," but of all the tasks she performed in this role, cooking was the most constant. Her novels, journalism, and nonfiction works are everywhere informed by her knowledge and love of food.

In Ellis' novels, food and the manners surrounding its preparation and consumption are a source of class identity and ill-feeling. The downtrodden Mrs. Mason (*The 27th Kingdom*) is forced to work in domestic service. She eats with a politeness that her bohemian employer, Irene, finds "grotesque." Protected by money and breeding from the need to use plate and napkin, Irene instead puts her elbows on the table, waves her fork to emphasize a point, and lets crumbs fall from her mouth. Ellis' characters are divided into those who cook and eat lustily, leaving the stems on spinach and using all of an animal, and those whose meals are prim and affected.

Ellis herself adopted the peasant style in her cooking and spent the extra time it afforded her drinking and reading. She was a champion of real food, using lashings of garlic and olive oil when they were still foreign objects sniffed at by most English cooks. With tongue firmly in cheek, she even descended to the production of *Darling, You Shouldn't Have Gone to So Much Trouble*, a cookbook for the housewife who has only ten minutes to prepare a meal. *Natural Baby Food* shows her in a more lavish mode, preparing meals to nourish and delight her many children and exhorting the nation to favor breastfeeding and homemade weaning food—advice that was, in 1977, still countercultural.

Recipes from her cookbooks find their way into the novels, just as the fictional use of food as dramatic device reappears in her polemical works as uncompromising censure. In *Fairy Tale*, the young Eloise trades London for rural Wales in order to commune with nature. But nature does not care for her—in fact, it wants to consume her. When the *Tylwyth Teg* use Eloise's body to incubate their changeling child, she abandons her vegetarianism and ends up deep in the wood, smeared in mud and filth, feeding on human flesh. Beware of paganism, Ellis warns; it isn't the comforting goddess so beloved of the New Age. It is dark, old, and dangerous; it gives license to the appetites that will leave us rotting in sins of the flesh.

Ellis knew that in both the religious house and the family home, the kitchen table ought to be counter-poised perfectly with the altar: earthly food needs to be real and sustaining and heavenly food properly refined by veneration. For Ellis, the changes wrought upon her beloved Tridentine Mass by the reformist spirit following the Second Vatican Council seemed like a desecration that turned the beauty and mystery of Christ's self-sacrifice into a casual meal.

The first translation of the Mass into English rendered the Latin description of transubstantiated wine, *potus spiritális*, to "spiritual drink." For Ellis, the "housewife," the word "drink" was deeply suspicious, a "word that manufacturers use when they want to put one over on you. . . . It is not the real thing." But very few in those early decades listened to her complaints. For decades Ellis took her fight to the closed doors of the liberal Catholic hierarchy, demanding, "Is it the blood of Christ or not?"[2] It was a thankless task. She lost friends and jobs and was harangued by letters and phone calls from heretics and atheists alike. When enough years had passed that Ellis' arguments weren't considered quite so heterodox, it was suggested by one mainstream

2. Ellis, 75.

newspaper that she be counted among the "revered guardians of the nation's conscience." She didn't want to be a moral guardian of the nation. "What," she asked, "has happened to those whose *job* it is" to mind the gates? "I don't mind doing my bit but I also have the housework to do."[3]

Before she died, Ellis completed *Fish, Flesh and Good Red Herring* (2004). It is a book about food, but it is also about writing. In fact, it realizes perfectly the wry everydayness that is Ellis' distinct "housewife" style, apparent to a greater or lesser extent in all her works. The reader walks with her from the kitchen to the bookshelf, where she rifles through the pages of Victorian recipe books before returning to the hob to stir the sauce and observe with arch acceptance the changes that have passed across the English table. Ellis' fiction and her journalism are similarly shaped: snatches of conversation overheard in the kitchen, copied hastily by the cook as she works. The narrative voice in so much of her writing is an echo of Ellis' inner thoughts as she passes opinion on the many voices that rose up in polyphony over her kitchen table. In fact, many of the most important scenes in her novels occur at the kitchen table.

Ellis' notebooks record this way of working: they are filled with hastily written observations in her own voice ("single-minded dedication to God is regarded as anti-social and possibly psychotic," "medical science is very inadequate," "people who believe in royalty are clinically insane") or the voice of one of her characters ("M thinks Seb's b and s in law bought each other at Harrods. Expensive, useless, top of the market"). These are interspersed with shopping items, phone numbers, prayers, and reminders ("put a lot of chat in the book" and "CALL SUE"). While the notebooks are clearly identifiable as private and unpolished texts, they nonetheless sound very similar to Ellis' anecdotal writing style, which manifests in the nonfiction and journalism as

---

3. Alice Thomas Ellis, *Cat Among the Pigeons* (London: HarperCollins, 1994), 1.

a string of loosely connected thoughts about subjects that seemed unremarkable until she turned to them, and in the fiction as the intimate internal meditations of a first-person narrator or the rapid eavesdropping of an omniscient storyteller as she circles through the rooms of a full house on a single day.

It is this quality of the homely and everyday that does in fact suggest a connection between Ellis' work and that of the Bloomsbury milieu—and not the work of the maternal Vanessa Bell (with whom Ellis, a painter before she was a writer, shared much in common) but of Virginia Woolf herself. In 1928, Woolf was asked to speak to the female students of Cambridge about "women and fiction"; the result was *A Room of One's Own*. It is a pillar in the feminist literary canon, but it is also a book about writing. It narrates the daily life of the writer when she is doing all the activities necessary for writing besides the putting of words on paper: time at the desk, time to think uninterrupted, time to drive "through London in an omnibus" or have "luncheon in a shop by herself." In this way, *A Room of One's Own* narrates the kind of life that, Woolf argues, a woman writer needs if she is to flourish. The reader is invited to follow Woolf as she wanders through London, economically free and unencumbered by family responsibilities, or stands at her bookshelf idling through various titles, turning an idea over in her mind.

The economic and familial independence that was for Woolf essential to a writer's freedom was anathema to the ever-busy Ellis, for whom housework was precisely the best form of writerly procrastination. She would dither at the Aga stove for a while, do some laundry, and prepare the dinner, her mind turning over the thing she needed to write. Then, like the louche woman she was not, she would lie on the couch with a packet of cigarettes watching an old movie, by which time she would be ready and the words would fall out in a torrent before anyone had time to wonder where she was. She too walked the reader through the bookcases, but she was thoroughly self-deprecating in her tastes.

She read Agatha Christie novels for their plot lines, Edwardian cookery books for their absurd advice, short stories for their brevity, the Bible for obvious reasons, and vast Victorian indexes of useless information for no reason at all. Of course, she read other things too but rarely mentioned them: poetry, Dickens, Shakespeare, folklore, letters from loved ones or from the dead.

Woolf asked, "What conditions are necessary for the creation of works of art?" and offered her own answer: "freedom." Ellis' answer, however, was "suffering." Two of her seven children died in her lifetime, and it was the death of her nineteen-year-old son, Joshua, that started her career as a novelist. He fell from the roof at Euston Station and lay in a coma for a year. Her notebooks from this time are heartbreaking. They record the process through which fiction writing emerged as the painfully logical result of her efforts to stay sane.

While Joshua lay in the hospital bed, as mysterious and unresponsive as a newborn baby, Ellis began taking notes for *The Birds of the Air*, in which the bereaved heroine acts on Ellis' own compulsion to follow her son into death. The prose of Ellis' own words to Josh merge into novelistic prose, her own grief helping her to shape the novel's character: "You were born in an orange painted room. No waters broke, a dry birth. It hurt a bit. Nothing like as much as it hurts now. How can you die without my permission? My dear child . . . COME BACK TO ME . . . She had lost interest in the exterior usual world that people took for granted. She knew and wished to know better another world that began inside herself but did not finish there."

Ellis' loss made her sadder, but it made her funnier too. And her ability to combine the deepest pathos with a jaunty wit makes her one of England's greatest, most accessible, and most moral ironists. She began a mid-1980s "Home Life" column by observing the merits of different tidying methods: one could pull everything out of the wardrobe, thus rendering it very tidy but leaving the hallway impassable. Or one could practice the Irish style: open the cupboard door gingerly, fling everything in, and then shut it quickly. But she concludes that one really oughtn't tidy at all because looking for a pair of gloves she would instead find a pair of her dead son's shoes and all the "grief comes flooding back, unchanged by time." How can their clothes "still be here when the people you love the best in the world have gone?"

In her own life, as in her novels, it was Ellis' friendships with other women that helped her to live with bereavement. With Caroline Blakemore and Beryl Bainbridge she could get drunk and laugh. But the friendship that structured her everyday experience was that of the indomitable Janet—nanny, secretary, driver, a regular character in the "Home Life" column, who also appeared in the novels under the guise of the steady, street-smart companion with criminal connections and a strong sense of family loyalty. Janet spent her life working for Ellis; from the age of twenty she would arrive in the morning and do whatever was needed: clean out the fridge, help cater for a lunch party, help pull the shopping basket through Camden Market, take the kids out, drive to Wales, type a manuscript, or just sit at the kitchen table and drink.

At Ellis' notorious parties, guests would gather in the hallways and sitting rooms, each hoping to receive a bit of Ellis' wit, but she would hover downstairs by the Aga with Janet and smoke, preferring the easy company of a familiar friend with whom to gossip. In her final notebook, written on her deathbed, there are snatches of thoughts about the past, lists in which she tries to find appropriate objects to leave her many loved ones, observations on dying ("The time may have arrived in my life when I can use the Exclamation Mark!"), and then, out of this muddle, the surprising: "I must try and understand (!) that Janet isn't coming with me.... I see her familiar, well-loved face at the barrier."

Ellis loved women in the way her husband, Colin, loved men: for their fellowship. He was happiest in his drawing room or at the high table with Horace, whiskey, and men of letters, as she was happiest, at least once the babies had grown up, drinking in the kitchen with smart and familiar women, either in London or in her preferred house in the Welsh countryside. While he edited classical scholarship and philosophy and professed to disdain the work of women novelists like those who sought Ellis' editorial acumen, she relished the writing of her female peers and predecessors: women who looked into the deepest horror of life's humiliations, its violence, and came up laughing.

Woolf's concern that women writers have no heritage comparable to that of men, no solid legacy of prominent women thinkers on whose knowledge and tradition they can draw, made little sense to Ellis. By the time she was writing there were certainly more women filling in those canonical shadows that so troubled Woolf, and yet from a Catholic perspective Woolf's proposition is untenable. Ellis' faith gave her a female history that her Protestant peers lacked: Catherine, Teresa, Julian, Edith, Elizabeth, Mary. "What is the most important event in women's history?" she was asked by one feminist interviewer. "The Annunciation."[4]

Late in her life, when her journalism was the most uncompromising, Ellis recalls of first-wave feminism: "Disgruntled females organized 'consciousness raising sessions' and adopted other outmoded and discredited Marxist tactics, so that in a while everyone hated them, though few dared to admit it. A dreadful breed of feminist men arose, claiming to sympathise with this struggle for justice, and everyone hated them too." Ellis mourned a womanhood that she had known in inter-war Liverpool: tough, funny, capable women, who could handle a scythe or smoke a pipe. She also mourned the womanhood of early Hollywood actresses: sharp-tongued, elegant, clever, feminine, and moral. "Katherine Hepburn, Joan Crawford, Bette Davis etc., none of whom resemble in the least the downtrodden wimps so crucial to the feminist myth."[5]

4. Cited in Damian Thompson, "Alice Doesn't Live Here Anymore," *Spectator*, March 19, 2005.

5. Ellis, *God Has Not Changed*, 1.

Ellis' most insistent argument with feminism was its en-croachment into Church doctrine and the movement for women's ordination, especially its arguments that women would cure any ills lurking in the Church. "Those who think women incapable of authoritarianism can never have met any. . . . Where in the world did they get the idea that women are not bossy? I have never met a man, no matter how patriarchal, who could outdo a determined woman in terms of sheer terror."[6] Her distaste with all the liberation movements of the 1960s was grounded in a deep concern over the rise of the "me" culture she saw all around her. Ellis believed that true freedom could only be found in giving oneself away—to children, to neighbors (in the widest sense), and ultimately to God.

Even in her final moments she was making something for her children. In her hospital bed, with second-stage lung cancer, she had no kitchen, no house, no paint with which to engage them. But she began a new notebook, filling it with thoughts for her daughter to read and comment upon once she was gone. Called "gardening in the dark," the small pages are a space in which Ellis and Sarah can continue their conversation, with each party on either side of the wall. This last, unfinished notebook makes painfully clear Ellis' insistent desire to observe and record and her knowledge that such a desire is ultimately fleeting. In life, there are observations through which the rapid passing of time can be caught—and shared. In death, there is only completeness.

> Even as I sit by the stream under the shade of the hawthorn, hand
> on the sun-warmed rock, watching the bees and the beetles and
> the birds doing concentratedly what they were conceived to do,
> feeling the grasses under my feet, and painstakingly identifying
> the wild flowers, I still cannot accept the moment for what it is.
> I know it will pass. Self-consciousness is the price we pay for the

6. Ellis, *Cat Among the Pigeons*, 53.

hope of immortality, and it is a high price. You put your hand in the stream and it runs through your fingers. You pick the flowers and they die. You hear the birds of this year but they are not the birds of last year, and next year they will be different birds. . . . It is perhaps easier to be sedated, to be bored, for at each moment of joyful consciousness comes the knowledge that it will pass; and as time passes, you realise it will never come again. It is more than that. It is an awareness that some of this world is so beautiful that it cannot be described; and, greedy and grasping as we are, we want not only to enjoy it but to tell it—so that it listens, and in listening becomes fixed—how unknowingly lovely it is. We look for a response from that which is unresponsive—for it takes no account of us. No wonder we dream of death, or a true consummation where longing ceases and the earth itself embraces us until we cannot be told apart, cannot be discerned, and have no responsibility.[7]

Making the everyday life of a woman into the stuff of fiction and nonfiction alike—that was Alice Thomas Ellis' great gift. She neither romanticized nor denigrated the life of the clever housewife and mother. In her company we can feel confident that the daily joys and drudgeries of family life matter, that they are not just a quiet and private pleasure but the stuff of literature, art, even of public life. With Ellis, the reader feels that the coming and going of friends and neighbors through the kitchen door, that the demands of feeding and dressing children, of dustbins and mailmen and household bills, are present as much in the life of one's own mind as they are in the life of the mind. For Woolf, freedom meant turning away from family life and the conventional expectations of women; for Ellis, it was precisely the conventional expectations that set her free.

7. Alice Thomas Ellis, *A Welsh Childhood* (London: Mermaid Books, 1990), 176–179.

RECOMMENDED READING

Fiction

Alice Thomas Ellis. *The 27th Kingdom.*
_____. *The Summer House: A Trilogy.*

Journalism

Alice Thomas Ellis. *God Has Not Changed.*

Bonnie Lander Johnson is Fellow and Associate Professor at Downing College, Cambridge University. Her academic books include *Chastity in Early Stuart Literature and Culture* and *Botanical Culture and Popular Belief in Shakespeare's England* (Cambridge University Press), *Blood Matters* (University of Pennsylvania Press), and *The Cambridge Handbook to Literature and Plants.* Her fiction and creative nonfiction have been published in *Hinterland*, *Howl*, and *Dappled Things* and shortlisted for The Royal Society of Literature's V.S. Pritchett Prize and The Brick Lane Bookshop Short Story Prize. With Julia Meszaros, she edits *Catholic Women Writers*, a Catholic University of America Press multivolume series that puts the women of the Catholic Literary Revival back into print.

Muriel Spark:
Transformative Satire

Dorian Speed

Half a century before Jim Carrey walked off the set of *The Truman Show* or Will Farrell negotiated with the novelist pulling the strings of his life story in *Stranger than Fiction*, Caroline Rose heard her own thoughts being typed out by an unseen author:

> A typewriter and a chorus of voices: What on earth are they up to at this time of night? Caroline wondered. But what worried her were the words they had used, coinciding so exactly with her own thoughts. Then it began again. Tap-tappity-tap; the typewriter. And again, the voices: Caroline ran out on to the landing, for it seemed quite certain the sound came from that direction. No one was there. The chanting reached her as she returned to her room, with these words exactly: What on earth are they up to at this time of night? Caroline wondered. But what worried her were the words they had used, coinciding so exactly with her own thoughts. And then the typewriter again: tap-tap-tap. She was rooted. "My God!" she cried aloud. "Am I going mad?"[1]

1. Muriel Spark, *The Comforters* (Philadelphia: Lippincot, 1957), 48.

Caroline's quest to identify the source of this ghostly narrator is just one plotline in Muriel Spark's debut novel, *The Comforters*. The 1957 publication of this book marked a radical departure from the dominant works of realistic fiction. Rather than dwell in the particular details of authenticity, Spark tips her hand to her readers and to Caroline early in the novel: "At this point in the narrative, it might be as well to state that the characters in this novel are all fictitious, and do not refer to any living persons whatsoever. Tap-tappity-tap."[2]

To read one of Spark's twenty-two novels or forty-one short stories is to hop through various moments in time, usually out of sequence, and often with foreknowledge of the final outcome. Her inventive use of "flash-forward" techniques may prove disorienting at first, while her willingness to playfully dispense miserable fates to her characters could be interpreted as capricious at best. Those expecting an anodyne procession of saintly protagonists from this Catholic author will be startled by the parade of petty egotists and hapless connivers who march through her collected works. Novelist and literary critic David Lodge has advised that "you really have to read it twice" to appreciate Spark's writing; given her characteristically efficient methods, this is an achievable and rewarding approach.[3] Her innovative techniques and the deeply moral framework that holds up her literary constructions set her apart from not only her secular peers but also many mainstream Catholic authors. Spark's own life story can provide context for her unconventional craft.

Born in 1918 to a Lithuanian Jewish father, Barney, and a Christian mother, Cissy, Muriel Camberg grew up in a "monument to religious eclecticism" in Edinburgh, Scotland.[4] Her

2. Spark, 75.

3. "Muriel Spark—the Elusive Spark," BBC Ex-S & BBC Bookmark Film, 1996.

4. Thomas Mallon, "Transfigured: How Muriel Spark Rose to Join the Crème de la Crème of British Fiction," *The New Yorker*, March 29, 2010, https://www.newyorker.com/magazine/2010/04/05/transfigured.

childhood allowed her to observe the vagaries of human nature through the various temporary lodgers in the Camberg home, while her education at Miss Gillespie's School for Girls formed her in Presbyterian teaching and inspired her most famous work, *The Prime of Miss Jean Brodie*. She was awarded "Queen of Poetry" in school and had for a mentor Miss Christina Kay, later refashioned drastically into the inimitable Brodie.[5] Her affection for her school days was of a piece with her belief that childhood was an "extraordinary, almost mystical time."[6] Throughout her career, she used the same school composition books for all of her writing, starting with the title and her name on the first page and taking off from there.

The Camberg family lacked the means to send Muriel to college, so she found work as a teacher and then as a secretary at a department store, a dull occupation except for the discount on clothes. Hoping for adventure, she abruptly departed Scotland at age nineteen for Southern Rhodesia with an eccentric mathematics teacher thirteen years her senior, Sydney Oswald Spark.

Muriel's time in Rhodesia was marked by the birth of her only son, Robin, and her first efforts to write poetry and stories. Her husband's initially erratic behavior escalated to violence and manipulation. He had courted her with promises to provide household servants so that she could concentrate on her writing, but upon their arrival he revealed that his relocation was due not to selflessness but to his inability to secure a job at home. She found herself isolated in a claustrophobic circle of white elites who reinforced one another in their racism. It was here, Spark wrote, that she "learned to keep in mind . . . the essentials of our

5. Muriel Spark, *Curriculum Vitae: A Volume of Autobiography* (New York: New Directions, 2011), 61. Spark wrote that she "felt like the Dairy Queen of Dumfries" and reports that her headmaster agreed that the crown was cheap-looking, like tinsel. Spark was pleased to receive a number of books to compensate for the "unsuitable nature of this coronet affair."

6. Ruth Whittaker, *The Faith and Fiction of Muriel Spark* (New York: St. Martin's, 1982), 43.

human destiny, our responsibilities, and to put in a peripheral place the personal sorrows, frights and horrors that came my way."[7] After her husband's violence escalated to beating her, they separated and eventually divorced. Muriel fled to Britain on a troop ship in 1944, reading T.S. Eliot while stacked four-deep in a bunk bed with other women, hoping to escape U-boat attacks. Her son, Robin, remained behind at a convent, since her husband had been awarded full custody and there was a wartime embargo on transporting children out of Africa.

Spark eventually won custody of her son, whom she sent to be raised by her parents while she established herself in London literacy circles. Her time working in the Foreign Office to forge passports and write propaganda has been described by biographer Martin Stannard as "project[ing] her into a fantastic world which became an image of the instability of literal truth."[8]

Spark found her footing as a literary critic and editor in the postwar period, working as editor of *The Poetry Review* from 1947 to 1949. In 1951, she published her first short story, "The Seraph and the Zambesi," inspired by a trip that she and her husband had taken to Victoria Falls along the Zambesi river in hopes of alleviating his deep depression. Spark reflected that their travels "gave me courage to endure the difficult years to come. The falls became to me a symbol of spiritual strength. I had no settled religion, but I recognized the experience . . . as spiritual in kind."[9]

As Spark's literary career was beginning in earnest, she embarked upon a relationship with fellow writer Derek Stanford that would end in acrimony, with Stanford writing an ill-advised biography of Spark and then finding himself lampooned in her 1998 novel *A Far Cry from Kensington*. Early in their time together, as Spark was beginning to correspond with T.S. Eliot, Evelyn

7. Spark, *Curriculum Vitae*, 113.

8. Martin Stannard, *Muriel Spark: The Biography* (New York: W.W. Norton, 2010), 101.

9. Spark, *Curriculum Vitae*, 122.

Waugh, and Graham Greene, she playfully asked Stanford, "Have you ever wanted to become a Catholic? I would if I could find Faith. I shall set out on a pilgrimage, I think, turning over small stones and leaves, climbing rare mountains in Tibet and making odd enquiries in public libraries, searching for Faith."[10]

This pilgrimage would lead Spark to the writings of St. John Henry Newman, which provided her not only a doctrinal understanding of Catholicism but the conviction she required to become a Catholic. Reticent about her interior life, Spark agreed with Newman that her conversion story was not "a thing one could propound 'between the soup and the fish' at a dinner party."[11] She saw a correspondence between the tenets of the faith and the truth that she had "always felt and known and believed," rather than experiencing a singular moment of revelation.[12] Her earlier time in Africa had prepared her for an appreciation of the mystery of human existence. These experiences, coupled with her intellectual acceptance of the faith, prompted her entry into the Roman Catholic Church in May 1954 after receiving instruction from Benedictine monk Dom Ambrose Agius.[13]

Spark's conversion and her emergence as an inventive new member of the mid-century literary scene were not merely co-incidental, in her eyes. She credited her conversion with greater freedom: "As a Catholic, I feel that nothing matters all that much . . . and so I was released in a liberated way."[14] Always intent on success, she now enjoyed the freedom of viewing her work from an eternal perspective—*sub specie aeternatis*. Her early stories

10. Letter from Muriel Spark to Derek Stanford, reprinted in Stannard, *Muriel Spark*, 101.

11. Spark, *Curriculum Vitae*, 201.

12. Spark, 201.

13. Spark, 202.

14. Muriel Spark, unpublished transcript of Granada Television interview with Malcolm Muggeridge, as cited in Whittaker, *The Faith and Fiction of Muriel Spark*, 42. In the interview, she said of her pre-conversion focus on professional success, "I didn't feel that I could grasp a subject and achieve it, because it mattered too much."

and novels often featured Catholic characters, although not necessarily in the most flattering of lights. In her later works, Catholicism might be mentioned obliquely but did not tend to overtly frame the story, even in *The Abbess of Crewe*, her 1974 satire of the Watergate scandal set in an English Benedictine abbey.

Throughout her life, Spark spoke very little about her conversion and the role of her faith in her work, but she asserted that it would be impossible for her not to remain a Catholic. In a 1998 episode of the literary review series *Booked*, eighty-year-old Spark debated the book of Job with Christopher Hitchens and then told interviewer David Aaronovitch, "You have to believe in the Holy Spirit . . . moving around the world. If you don't believe in that, then you don't believe in anything. Life is a mystery."[15]

Literary critics disagree as to how much correlation exists between Spark's techniques and her Catholicism. Ruth Whittaker, author of *The Faith and Fiction of Muriel Spark*, has argued that Spark differs radically from the kitchen sink realist writers of Britain in the 1950s, who conveyed reality as accurately as possible without conferring value or significance.[16] Rather than heroic protagonists who transcend the confines of class and social standing, Spark's characters find themselves fixed within plots, either of their own making or at the hands of other manipulators. Whittaker believes this reflected the growing belief that the twentieth century was "too bizarre to fit within realist conventions," but Spark's schemes do not reflect arbitrary dispensing of suffering upon her characters.[17] Instead, a consistent moral structure supports her stories, one in which their subtle falsehoods and self-deceptions lead to ruin.

---

15. "Booked (May 1998)—Muriel Spark, Christopher Hitchens and Nigella Lawson," BBC Channel Four, 1998, https://www.youtube.com /watch?v=eVLqjA98cFA.

16. Whittaker, *The Faith and Fiction of Muriel Spark*, 6.

17. Whittaker, 6.

The Comforters established Muriel Spark as a singular talent, employing the fanciful conceit of a narrator typing out the fate of a protagonist tied loosely to a smuggling ring under highly unlikely leadership. Evelyn Waugh wrote in a review titled "Something Fresh" that the book "came to me just as I had finished a story on a similar theme and I was struck by how much more ambitious was Miss Spark's essay and how much better she had accomplished it."[18] In a bizarre coincidence, both Waugh and Spark had suffered bouts of hallucinations related to drug poisoning; Waugh from using bromide as a sedative, and Spark from relying upon over-the-counter amphetamines widely used as stimulants and appetite suppressants. Spark's symptoms of psychosis were recognized by her friends when she began to insist that T.S. Eliot was sending her encrypted messages in his plays, which she was studying as a critic. She recovered with the help of her physician and the support of Waugh, Graham Greene, and Eliot toward her recuperation.

While the circumstances of her own addiction and recovery directly inspired the plight of the fictional Caroline Rose in *The Comforters*, the true source of meaning for this work was the book of Job. The title refers to the inept attempts of Job's friends and family to convince him that the suffering meted out to him must be in response to his particular sins. Spark had read the story of Job in primary school and remained fascinated by it throughout her life, particularly the poetry through which God reveals his transcendent command of creation.[19] God's handiwork and his pervasiveness are more than the human mind can comprehend, and his providence is superior to our foolish attempts to master our own fates.

18. Evelyn Waugh, "Something Fresh," *Spectator*, February 22, 1957, 256, quoted in Stannard, *Muriel Spark*, 179.

19. "Booked (May 1998)—Muriel Spark, Christopher Hitchens and Nigella Lawson."

Spark often employs a "God-like" narrative voice in her work, in which characters are described from a remote perspective without much exploration of their interior lives. In a review of Spark's autobiographical *Curriculum Vitae*, Roger Kimball remarked that she "recounts the menu but doesn't attempt to describe the meal" with regard to her spiritual life, and this descriptor could also apply to her economical prose.[20] She quickly paints characters with the lightest of touches but captures them so well that their actions (generally malevolent) toward one another are perfectly in keeping with what she has described. To recognize oneself in a Sparkian tale is therefore deeply unsettling.

The Comforters launched an intensely productive period for Spark, in which she authored a novel each year from 1957 until 1961. Her experimentation with form and technique flourished in short novels such as *Memento Mori*, in which a group of elderly upper-class Britons are informed "Remember you must die" via a mysterious phone caller. As her literary reputation developed, critics were unsure how to evaluate her. "This is a fascinating moment in the life of Muriel Spark," the *Standard* noted, "a moment when the world, having been blankly indifferent for years, suddenly begins to applaud and reward her."[21] She would soon step fully into the limelight with the 1961 publication of her most well-known work, *The Prime of Miss Jean Brodie*.

Brodie was inspired by Spark's childhood at James Gillespie's High School for Girls, where her intellect and imagination were formed. The fictitious schoolgirls of the Marcia Blaine School who comprise the "Brodie set" are mentored and manipulated by the formidable Jean Brodie, who anoints herself with the mission of "putting old heads on your young shoulders . . . and all my

20. Roger Kimball, "The First Half of Muriel Spark," *The New Criterion*, April 1993, https://newcriterion.com/issues/1993/4/the-first-half-of-muriel-spark.

21. As quoted in Stannard, *Muriel Spark*, 228.

pupils are the crème de la crème."²² Spark reveals early in the novel that one of the young women has "betrayed" Miss Brodie, their self-appointed idol, and the remainder of the story weaves the fates of each pupil together with the disturbing schemes and principles of their teacher. Adapted for the stage in 1966, it was the basis of a 1969 movie for which Maggie Smith earned an Academy Award. Scottish Television later produced a seven-part serialization of the novel, which Spark considered the better adaptation.

For her next work, *The Girls of Slender Means*, Spark drew upon her experiences in postwar London to portray another group of young women linked by circumstance. The residents of the May of Teck Club live together in a hostel reserved for single women in pursuit of vocations during the final days of the Second World War. What begins as a clever romp through their love lives and professional aspirations becomes a deeper exploration of suffering and sinfulness, propelled by the question of how the anarchist intellectual and sometime-paramour of one of the young women ended up as a Jesuit murdered in Haiti.

Brodie and *Slender Means* are standout examples of one of Spark's signature methods: the narrative leaps ahead in time, often parenthetically, to reveal what will ultimately become of a character. Spark's narrators and characters foretell grisly deaths, lurid affairs, and all manner of crimes. When asked by interviewer Robert Hosmer if this device functioned to direct the reader's attention temporarily away from plot, Spark replied that it serves a dual function. While "giving the show away in a strange manner creates suspense more than the withholding of information," she also considered this device to have an "eschatological function."²³

22. Muriel Spark, *The Prime of Miss Jean Brodie* (Edinburgh: Barrington Stoke, 2020). These words are repeated by Miss Brodie throughout the novel.

23. Robert Hosmer and Muriel Spark, "An Interview with Dame Muriel Spark," *Salmagundi*, no. 146/147 (2005): 150.

Ruth Whittaker has asserted that "reality (for Spark) lies not in the novel nor in the everyday world, but in the realm of God."[24]

Spark traveled alone to the Holy Land for four weeks in the summer of 1961, a journey motivated by her Jewish heritage as much as by her conversion to Christianity. It was a harrowing trip, particularly since she began by observing portions of the trial of Nazi war criminal Adolf Eichmann in Jerusalem. Biographer Martin Stannard describes her sadness and sense of displacement upon returning from the trip; anti-Semitism was familiar to her from her own family's experiences, and she was repulsed by Eichmann's self-assurance at the trial. Yet "there was perhaps another nagging sensation which she was supposed not to feel: that there was something pernicious in this desire to crush so pathetic an object of hatred, a self-righteousness she had always resisted."[25] Her travels inspired the short story "The Gentile Jewess" and her next novel, *The Mandelbaum Gate.*

The next five novellas—*The Public Image, The Driver's Seat, Not to Disturb, The Hothouse by the East River,* and *The Abbess of Crewe*—mark a slight departure in theme and technique, with a decided focus on "the exposure of fictions," as Ruth Whittaker observes.[26] Spark had an ear for jargon and posturing and a fascination with characters who hope to control their own narratives, dispatching consequences to them despite their best efforts to fake their way through situations.

The Driver's Seat was the novel that Spark considered her best work, and it is also perhaps the novel most likely to shock and scandalize readers. Spark had read a newspaper account of a grisly murder in which a young woman had been actively seeking someone who would pursue her as a potential victim; the young man "went too far in the game" and was sentenced to prison for several years. Spark was "fascinated with what sort of girl . . .

24. Whittaker, *The Faith and Fiction of Muriel Spark,* 11.

25. Stannard, *Muriel Spark,* 245.

26. Whittaker, *The Faith and Fiction of Muriel Spark,* 12.

would do this" and rewrote the story as a "whydunit" from the point of view of the victim, Lise.[27] Although, as is typical of Spark's work, the ending is revealed ahead of time, the spiritual bleakness is still a shock to the system. Spark agreed that she took a "very cold approach" in this and other works, but she explained in an interview with David Lodge that she alerts the reader at the close of the story that polite society fails in avoiding "exposure of fear and pity, pity and fear"—the necessary components of tragedy.[28]

Although Spark does not linger excessively on the gore and wretchedness she inflicts upon her characters, this should not be interpreted as a moral neutrality. In a 1996 diary entry on Slate.com, she writes about her habit of reading the Bible "as literature, as history, as a source of wisdom":

> Another of my favorite proverbs lists a number of human attributes detestable to God, with which I quite agree (Proverbs 6, 16-19):
>
> *These six things doth the Lord hate: yea, seven are an abomination unto him: A proud look, a lying tongue, and hands that shed innocent blood. An heart that deviseth wicked imaginations, feet that be swift in running to mischief, a false witness that speaketh lies, and he that soweth discord among brethren.*[29]

One could easily draw up a checklist of these attributes and mark them off as each appears in a Sparkian tale, particularly the devising of wicked imaginations. "'People fail you' is the message of her novels . . . almost mitigated by her assurances that God does not," Whittaker observes.[30]

27. "Muriel Spark—the Elusive Spark."

28. In her BBC interview with David Lodge, Spark identifies this as Aristotle's definition of tragedy.

29. Muriel Spark, "Diary—Dame Muriel Spark," *Slate Magazine*, December 14, 1996, https://slate.com/human-interest/1996/12/dame-muriel-spark-2.html.

30. Whittaker, *The Faith and Fiction of Muriel Spark*, 36.

These assurances of God's providence tend to disappear more and more into the subtext of Spark's later works, in which Catholicism rarely figures and then only as an apparently secondary aspect of a character or situation.

Thomas Mallon summed up Spark's general formula in a 2010 New Yorker article: "With a few variations, your Sparkian heroine will be an ... intensely clever woman, an editor or a writer, a bit lonely, a bit criminally inclined ... a watchful woman talented at teasing out secrets. Put simply: imagine the young Muriel Spark."[31] Indeed, the author returned to semi-faithful portrayals of herself in later books *A Far Cry from Kensington* and *Loitering with Intent*. As in *The Comforters*, the protagonist of *Loitering*, Fleur Talbot, discovers overlap between her novel-in-progress and the events of her own life; she believes that "seeing people as they were" is critical to her success as a writer, and that a novelist who correctly perceives a character can thereby predict their behavior.[32]

Vice has a trajectory in the world of Muriel Spark, and it will eventually lead to suffering, whether intentional or not. This stark approach can seem at first like the author is withholding judgment on the morality of a character's actions. Spark firmly avoided sentimentality in her fiction, believing that providing readers with a cathartic experience of having participated in suffering and its resolution would offer them a feeling of having fulfilled their moral duties. She agreed that God could be considered "a character by omission" in her works; the resulting absence allows for her to document how foolish our pretensions to self-determination and how deep our attraction to vice. Spark admitted that her distant approach to the actions and words of her characters might be insufficient for some to glean the proper moral understanding: "Readers are a very meagre species."[33]

31. Mallon, "Transfigured."

32. Muriel Spark, *Loitering with Intent* (New York: New Directions, 2014), 10.

33. Muriel Spark, interview with Ian Gillham, BBC World Service program *Writers of Today*, quoted in Whittaker, *The Faith and Fiction of Muriel Spark*, 149.

Helena Tomko has identified a subtle thread that runs through much of Spark's fiction and leads the reader beyond the text itself into transcendent mystery. Within many of her stories and novels, Spark has characters quote other works—Scripture, poetry, popular songs—that speak to a greater reality. Tomko has written of Spark's usage of Gerard Manley Hopkins' poem "The Wreck of the Deutschland" in *The Girls of Slender Means*, where it serves as a practice text for elocution lessons. She recognizes this as "a private conversation between text and reader, where meaning bids farewell to satire and seeks out the company of poetry, scripture, and prayer."[34]

Once alerted to this technique, a reader can remain on the alert for other intimations of grace in Spark's fiction. The mystery of the Transfiguration is central to the adult life of one of the girls in the "Brodie set" and appears repeatedly as what Jonathan Coe has termed the "hypnotic recurrence" of an idea or work that a character mentions almost as a litany.[35] The protagonist of *The Mandelbaum Gate* recites, "We have an everlasting city, but not here; our goal is the city that is one day to be."[36] In her 1976 novel *The Takeover*, Spark has a character recite St. Paul's condemnation of the worship of Diana from the Acts of the Apostles in response to another character's efforts to revive her cult. As easy as it is to zoom through Spark's clean, energetic prose, readers should keep a steady lookout for these faint signals of her true purpose.

Spark died at the age of eighty-eight in Tuscany in 2006, where she had taken up residence with her friend and literary executor Penelope Jardine in the 1970s. She had refused to allow biographer Martin Stannard to publish his work during her lifetime, and it was only after both she and later Jardine had

34. Helena M. Tomko, "Muriel Spark's *The Girls of Slender Means* at the Limits of the Catholic Novel," *Religion & Literature* 47, no. 2 (2015): 57.

35. Jonathan Coe, "Conversions," *London Review of Books*, September 13, 1990, https://www.lrb.co.uk/the-paper/v12/n17/jonathan-coe/conversions.

36. Muriel Spark, *The Mandelbaum Gate* (New York: Knopf, 1965), 235.

gone through to "make it a bit fairer" that it came to market in 2009.[37] In her lifetime, she enjoyed tremendous acclaim over the decades, awarded Officer of the Order of the British Empire in 1967 and Dame Commander of the Order of the British Empire in 1993 for services to literature. Several of her works earned honors, including two nominations for the Booker Prize.

New readers may enjoy beginning with her collected short stories, which span her full literary career and draw especially upon her experiences in Africa. Stannard's biography, however poorly received by Spark herself, captures the drama of her remarkable life and provides insights into her various works. *The Prime of Miss Jean Brodie* and *The Girls of Slender Means* have both enjoyed tremendous popularity, while more recent works such as *The Symposium* read like they could have been written in the last year, so modern are their concerns.

Spark's uniqueness lies in her inventive techniques, her implications of grace, and her sharply satirical takes on what David Lodge called "continental scandal sheets turned into literature."[38] On her determination to portray the workings of God *sub specie aeternatis* instead of holding her readers' hands through morality lessons, she offers:

> I don't ever say that there is something mysterious going on here. I try not to hope that all this other dimension is sort of read between the lines, and I think that effect can be achieved in a purely methodical and technical way by keeping out as much comment as possible.[39]

37. Tim Walker, quoting Spark's friend A.S. Byatt in his article "Companion Shelves 'Unfair' Spark Biography," *The Telegraph*, April 22, 2007, https://www.telegraph.co.uk/news/uknews/1549332/Companion-shelves-unfair-Spark-biography.html.

38. "Muriel Spark—the Elusive Spark."

39. Muriel Spark, unpublished transcript of Granada Television interview with Malcolm Muggeridge, as cited in Whittaker, *The Faith and Fiction of Muriel Spark*, 134.

RECOMMENDED READING

Fiction

Muriel Spark. *The Abbess of Crewe.*
_____. *All the Stories of Muriel Spark.*
_____. *The Comforters.*
_____. *The Driver's Seat.*
_____. *The Girls of Slender Means.*
_____. *Loitering with Intent.*
_____. *The Mandelbaum Gate.*
_____. *Memento Mori.*
_____. *The Prime of Miss Jean Brodie.*
_____. *The Public Image.*

Memoir

Muriel Spark. *Curriculum Vitae.*
_____. *The Informed Air: Essays.*

Other

Martin Stannard. *Muriel Spark: The Biography.*
Ruth Whittaker. *The Faith and Fiction of Muriel Spark.*

Dorian Speed is a writer, educator, and speaker living outside Houston. For the past twenty years, she has taught middle and high school students in a variety of settings. She is currently working on a book comparing Flannery O'Connor and Muriel Spark, along with her first novel.

Toni Morrison:
Writer of the Crucifix

Nick Ripatrazone

The cover of the 1948 Lorain High School yearbook reads "The Best Years of Our Lives" in gold-embossed letters against a red background. At the time of printing, 1,467 students were enrolled in the school—including a talented junior named Chloe Wofford. She was active in several academic and social activities. She stands proud in the front row of the A Capella Choir, a sash adorned with an *L* draped over her shoulders. Her mother sang in the choir at the Greater St. Matthew A.M.E. Church in Lorain; in fact, her mother seemed to always be singing—no matter what she was doing.

Wofford served on the Student Senate-Council. The next year, as a senior, she held the position of Treasurer, and helped plan campus events. She was on the staff of the *Hi-Standard*, the bi-weekly student newspaper. She wrote and edited features for the publication. She worked as an aide at the school's library, where her tasks included checking out books to students and repairing old and worn texts.

After school, she worked as the secretary to the head librarian at the main branch of the Lorain Public Library. Nearly forty years later, her hometown debated how best to honor the first black woman to win the Nobel Prize in Literature—and to this day, the only American Catholic woman to win the prize. Some suggested a statue; others a park or a street named for her.

The woman who was being honored had her own idea. It would be most appropriate, she said, for a single room to bear her name. A room with "comfortable, upholstered chairs," where young readers could "make their own acquaintance with books."[1] Books, the Nobel Prize winner affirmed, matter. "Books are intellectually challenging. Books make you confront things. They make you discover things that would have gone undiscovered."[2]

The Toni Morrison Reading Room was dedicated on January 22, 1995. It is a small but uniquely special honor for a transcendent artist, a woman whose fiction bears witness to suffering and joy.

Toni Morrison was born Chloe Ardelia Wofford on February 18, 1931, in Lorain, Ohio, a steel town on the shore of Lake Erie. Less than a decade before her birth, the deadliest tornado in state history tore through the town, killing seventy-two people and decimating businesses, churches, and homes. The town battled back, but residents carried the memory that everything could be lost in an instant.

Her parents were George and Ramah Wofford; they were originally from Georgia and Alabama. Morrison grew up attending the St. Matthew Methodist Church with her family. She was moved by her mother's voice; church, Morrison said, was primarily her mother and music. Outside of church, her mother and other family members "talked a great deal about Jesus."[3] Morrison, who learned to read well at an early age—so well that she was often selected to read aloud to other students—was especially attuned

1. "Toni Morrison Room History," Lorain Public Library, https://www.lorainpubliclibrary.org/locations-hours/main-library/toni-morrison-room.

2. "Toni Morrison Room History."

3. Danielle Taylor-Guthrie, ed., *Conversations with Toni Morrison* (Jackson: University Press of Mississippi, 1994), 115.

to the *language* of faith. She noticed that when her family spoke of serious matters, their manner was "highly sermonic, highly formalized, biblical in a sense."[4] Her Methodist family could "move easily into the language of the King James Bible and then back to standard English, and then segue into language that we would call street. It was seamless, and this was extremely attractive to me to hear."[5] Both the content and manner of their speech were formative for her.

Equally formative was the fact that her family "took [religion] very, very seriously, so it would be very difficult for me not to."[6] Yet even as a child, Morrison noticed that her family "kept this other body of knowledge that we call superstitious."[7] She was surrounded by stories and storytellers; her father would tell ghost stories each night. Morrison described black storytelling tradition as a process that is similar to midrash, the Jewish rabbinical tradition of deeply interpreting and reconsidering biblical narratives to see them anew: a way of "cleaning up the language so that old words have new meanings."[8] The "spine" of black storytelling is "very biblical and meandering and aural—you really have to hear it."[9]

Young Morrison, smart and curious, was surrounded by belief and story—and yet the sense of preternatural mystery that might have connected to the two elements seemed absent. Other than her mother's voice, she was not moved by Methodist services; she much preferred the supernatural storytelling of home. Into that absence arrived the influence of her cousin, "a fervent Catholic."[10] A part of Morrison's family was Roman Catholic, and Morrison

4. Carolyn C. Denard, ed., *Toni Morrison: Conversations* (Jackson: University Press of Mississippi, 2008), 59.

5. Denard, 131.

6. Taylor-Guthrie, *Conversations*, 178.

7. Taylor-Guthrie, 115.

8. Taylor-Guthrie, 136.

9. Taylor-Guthrie, 136.

10. Antonio Monda, *Do You Believe?* (New York: Vintage, 2007), 117.

began attending Mass. She became transfixed by the "aesthetics" of the Latin Rite—no surprise for a gifted young woman who longed for powerful stories.[11]

At twelve years old, Morrison converted to Catholicism. She took the name of St. Anthony of Padua—Anthony becoming her middle name—and her nickname soon became Toni. Family and close friends would still call her Chloe, but the name Toni stuck.

At the same time Morrison was cultivating her love for books and language as a high school student—she took four years of Latin—she was also "fascinated by the rituals of Catholicism."[12] Her choice of words is noteworthy. Morrison was not merely a believer; she was intellectually and aesthetically drawn to Catholicism. Years later, Morrison would recall that she had "a moment of crisis on the occasion of Vatican II."[13] She "suffered greatly from the abolition of Latin, which I saw as the unifying and universal language of the Church."[14]

In addition to her intelligence and curiosity, Morrison was a hard worker, something she learned from her parents. Along with her responsibilities as a homemaker, her mother worked as a custodian in the Lorain schools and at the American Stove Company—a factory that produced stoves, heaters, and furnaces. "I was surrounded by black women who were very tough and very aggressive and who always assumed they had to work and rear children and manage homes," she wrote.[15] "They had enormously high expectations of their daughters, and cut no quarter with us."[16] Her father was a welder who worked on ships. Morrison saw that their work ethic was inextricable from their sense of pride.

11. Terry Gross, "I Regret Everything," NPR, August 24, 2015, https://www.npr.org/2015/08/24/434132724/i-regret-everything-toni-morrison-looks-back-on-her-personal-life.

12. Monda, *Do You Believe?*, 117.

13. Monda, 118.

14. Monda, 118.

15. Denard, *Toni Morrison*, 142.

16. Denard, 142.

She said that although she "always knew we were very poor," her parents "made all of us feel as though there were these rather extraordinary deserving people within us."[17] She recalled that her father came home one day from work and exclaimed, "Today I welded a perfect seam and I signed my name to it."[18] Young Morrison responded that no one would actually see his signature on the ship. Yes, her father responded, "but I know it's there."[19]

Morrison channeled that intrinsic drive as a student. She was aware of her family's joy and fortitude despite their struggles and was comfortable among the surrounding Irish, Italian, and Eastern European immigrant families. The "racial and ethnic mix" in Lorain "was so tight and so unhostile."[20] In her fiction and nonfiction, Morrison would make it a point to render similar spaces of black residency: "There are hundreds of small towns and that's where most black people live."[21] In a 1991 speech at Oberlin College, Morrison would say that for her entire life, the process of imagining her work "always starts right here on the lip of Lake Erie."[22]

After graduating high school in 1949, Morrison attended Howard University in Washington, DC, where she studied literature and theater. She graduated in 1953 and completed an MA in English literature at Cornell in Ithaca, New York. Her concluding thesis was titled "Virginia Woolf's and William Faulkner's Treatment of the Alienated." She said that Faulkner was "brilliant" at imagining black people in his writing, the "only writer who took black people seriously."[23]

17. Denard, 100.

18. Denard, 100.

19. Denard, 100.

20. Denard, 131.

21. Taylor-Guthrie, *Conversations*, 12.

22. Jennifer Haliburton, "Remembering Toni Morrison," Ohio Magazine, August 2019, https://www.ohiomagazine.com/arts/article/remembering-toni-morrison.

23. Denard, *Toni Morrison*, 101.

In the decade that followed, Morrison taught at Texas Southern University and at Howard, married, had two sons, and divorced—pausing her teaching career for editorial work at Random House. She would continue editing for two decades. "What I enjoyed most was line editing, working the actual text," she noted, but she had a significant career in acquiring books and mentoring writers.[24] She published Muhammad Ali, Toni Cade Bambara, Angela Davis, and Chinua Achebe, among others.

Her own debut novel, *The Bluest Eye*, appeared in 1970, followed by *Sula* (1973), *Song of Solomon* (1977), and *Tar Baby* (1981). Yet *Beloved*, arriving in 1987, is her towering achievement—and her most Catholic book. Although nuns flit across the first page in *The Bluest Eye*, *Beloved* is the pinnacle of Morrison's literary and emotional journey as a black Catholic in America. It is a book that reckons with the horrors of slavery and its aftermath, a story of God-created bodies and souls whose labors and loves haunt the pages.

For Morrison, Catholicism was an absolutely visceral, corporeal religion, a faith of bodies. Morrison meditated upon her Catholic identity in a 2004 conversation with Cornel West, who typically introduced Morrison as a Catholic writer. West noted that Morrison, in the vein of Flannery O'Connor, "has an incarnational conception of human existence."[25] During their conversation, Morrison offered a useful image through which we can understand her literary and personal Catholicism.

"Now, you know, I'm a Catholic," Morrison said, "so we're used to blood and gore. On the cross in the church, there's the body, with the cuts and the bruises. Protestant churches: nice, clean cross. No body at all."[26] Later the conversation turned to

24. Denard, 204.

25. "Dorothy Day as Known by Cornel West," YouTube video, March 16, 2014, https://www.youtube.com/watch?v=dHo2QArOaq4.

26. "Conversation with Cornel West," C-SPAN Video, March 24, 2004, https://www.c-span.org/video/?181101-1/conversation-cornel-west.

the recently released film *The Passion of the Christ*. Although Morrison critiqued the overly bloody nature of the extended torture sequence, she used the film as an opportunity to contemplate how the Passion itself was "really about the flesh."[27] She lamented that "we forget that" physicality—that humanity—of Christ. "This is real suffering," she said.[28] "I was looking at it like a lynching. . . . This is a betrayed man who is hung, lynched."[29]

These are moving, public, profoundly Catholic meditations on Christ, and they are coming from a Nobel Laureate. Yet Morrison's identity as a Catholic is largely unknown, or perhaps ignored. The former possibility might be a result of a secular culture of criticism that is ill-equipped to detect or wrangle with her Catholicism. Critics who justifiably laud her work fail to engage with its religious anchoring, and that absence is a missed opportunity.

The latter possibility for the ignorance of Morrison's Catholic identity, though, is more concerning. As the screenwriter Myles Connolly once noted, Catholics love nothing more than to laud the artistic accomplishments of one of their ilk. For years, Catholic critics have mined the latent Catholicism of writers, singers, and artists. Yet somehow, Morrison's Catholicism has remained untouched. Her Catholicism is a mere biographical footnote, an explanation for her first name.

How is it possible that the first American-born Catholic to win the Nobel since Ernest Hemingway is unengaged as a Catholic novelist? Morrison's work challenges readers—at the levels of both language and content. Her rich, poetic writing is experimental in syntax and scope. She deeply inhabits the worlds of her stories, and whether a scene is written in the narrated voice of a character or from a third-person view, it hews close to the atmosphere of

27. "Conversation with Cornel West."
28. "Conversation with Cornel West."
29. "Conversation with Cornel West."

the scene. In short, Morrison writes powerfully—and that power can shake a reader.

Morrison's work is not for the complacent—and yet the Church compels us to bear visceral witness in much the same tone as she did on the page. One might liken Morrison's atmosphere to the communal reading of the Passion at Mass; when we look away from Christ's suffering on the cross, we lessen its efficacy in our lives.

Beloved, then, is the perfect entry point to encounter Morrison's deeply Catholic vision. The novel takes place in Morrison's home state in the years after the Civil War. A woman named Sethe has fled slavery but remains haunted by her abuse and her own great sin: she killed her infant child, motivated by fear that her daughter would be caught and enslaved. The act, so nightmarish as to feel unreal, permeates the book. Such savagery will likely challenge Catholic readers—but the revelations that follow make the reading deeply worthwhile and moving.

Morrison's earliest sense of story was formed through religion and the ghost tales shared by her family at night. *Beloved* brings them together in the book, starting with a haunting epigraph from Romans 9:25: "I will call them my people, / which were not my people; / and her beloved, / which was not beloved." The quote is enigmatic in sense and recursive in style. Here Paul in Romans actually quotes Hosea 2:23—immediately establishing *Beloved* as a book that calls us back to other stories. In fact, the titular character is herself someone who calls back the past, doing so in flesh and blood.

When Beloved mysteriously arrives at Sethe's home at 124 Bluestone Road in Cincinnati, emerging from a stream, her skin "lineless and smooth,"[30] she has already been prophesied. Denver, Sethe's young daughter, had been fascinated by a "baby ghost"—a mischievous spirit that attacked their home. Denver, who often

---

30. Toni Morrison, *Beloved* (New York: Plume, 1988), 50.

saw Sethe on her knees in prayer, had seen the ghost kneel down next to her.[31]

Now, Beloved has arrived, the spirit of the child long gone. Her voice is "so low and rough."[32] She shares a name with Sethe's deceased baby. She longs for stories of the past. Her obsession with Sethe is dangerous; it feels like the preface to revenge.

In the woods near their home, Sethe's mother-in-law, Baby Suggs, had journeyed "to the Clearing—a wide-open place cut deep in the woods nobody knew for what at the end of a path known only to deer and whoever cleared the land in the first place. In the heat of every Saturday afternoon, she sat in the clearing while the people waited among the trees."[33] Her preaching became charismatic, and years later, that spirit compels Sethe to return to that place. "Before the light changed," Morrison writes, "while it was still the green blessed place she remembered: misty with plant steam and the decay of berries."[34]

As the novel builds toward a conclusion, it is another congregation of women who make a pilgrimage to Sethe's home. They pray, and then they sing—the religious language that first formed Morrison: "It was as though the Clearing had come to her with all its heat and simmering leaves, where the voices of women searched for the right combination, the key, the code, the sound that broke the back of words. Building voice upon voice until they found it, and when they did it was a wave of sound wide enough to sound deep water and knock the pods of chestnut trees. It broke over Sethe and she trembled like the baptized in its wash."[35]

Beloved is a novel of the crucifix: of unspeakable sins that must be spoken of, for that is how healing occurs. Catholic liturgical life is seasonal; we return to old stories and renew those ancient truths. Rather than avoid the suffering of Christ, Catholics devote

31. Morrison, 13.
32. Morrison, 52.
33. Morrison, 87.
34. Morrison, 89.
35. Morrison, 261.

forty days to deep spiritual preparation for the celebration of Easter. *Beloved* is a Lenten read, a book to ponder, to struggle with, to emerge from more fully aware of how Christ's bodily suffering is reflected in the worn and weary bodies of our own world.

Morrison's books typically do not contain Catholic characters, but Catholic readers know—from Flannery O'Connor's masterful fiction—that an incarnational vision of the world needs to look everywhere. Although another novel by Morrison, *Paradise*, does include Catholic nuns, the words of a Baptist preacher most reverberate with a Catholic vision within that book. He contemplates the eternal, universal symbol of Christ's cross. Yet it is the *body* on the cross that is most essential, the man "propped up on these two intersecting lines to which he was attached in a parody of human embrace, fastened to two big sticks that were so convenient, so recognizable, so embedded in consciousness as consciousness, being both ordinary and sublime."[36]

He describes Christ at Calvary: "His woolly head alternately rising on his neck and falling toward his chest, the glow of his midnight skin dimmed by dust, streaked by gall, fouled by spit and urine, gone pewter in the hot, dry wind and, finally, as the sun dimmed in shame, as his flesh matched the odd lessening of afternoon light as though it were evening, always sudden in that climate, swallowing him and the other death row felons, and the silhouette of this original sin merged with a false night sky."[37]

Toni Morrison was a writer of the crucifix, of a God who became man and, in doing so, saves us all—embraces us all. Her religious vision was scorching, not sentimental; challenging, not saccharine. Despite her clear talent and cultural significance, Morrison's books have been banned by some school districts and labeled as dangerous. This censorship is unfortunate and misguided. Morrison's work has the capacity to make its readers uncomfortable not because she sought to be profane or shocking.

36. Toni Morrison, *Paradise* (New York: Vintage, 2014), 146.
37. Morrison, 146.

Rather, Morrison's work is deeply, almost disarmingly human—in all of our foibles and sins. Morrison was bearing a Catholic witness to the world, and to silence her work is to stifle an essential American Catholic voice.

Morrison preferred uncomfortable truths to complacency. Although she had criticisms for the Church, those criticisms arose from a deep respect for the life and suffering of Christ. As recently as 2015, she said that although she was a "lapsed Catholic," "Pope Francis is impressive enough to make me reconsider my error."[38] In other interviews around that time, she eschewed the *lapsed*, instead affirming that she was a Catholic. The vacillation should not be seen as surprising. Morrison took religion seriously—and seriousness breeds contemplation and even doubt. She lamented the absence of authentic religion in much of modern art: "It's not serious—it's supermarket religion, a spiritual Disneyland of false fear and pleasure."[39] In contrast to that superficiality, her own work is a revelation.

RECOMMENDED READING

Toni Morrison. *Beloved.*

_____. *The Bluest Eye.*

_____. *Paradise.*

_____. *Song of Solomon.*

_____. *Sula.*

Nick Ripatrazone is the Culture Editor for the journal *Image* and a Contributing Editor for the *Catholic Herald* (UK). His recent books include *Longing for an Absent God* and *The Habit of Poetry: The Literary Lives of Nuns in Mid-century America.*

38. Neanda Salvaterra, "The Pope in America: Voices," *The Wall Street Journal*, September 21, 2015, https://graphics.wsj.com/image-grid/pope-francis-in-US-2015/.

39. Monda, *Do You Believe?*, 121.

Alice McDermott:
Radiant Vision in *Someone*

Paul J. Contino

DESCENT INTO THE FINITE

Alice McDermott writes like a saint. Her narrative art offers her readers a sense of participatory wholeness with the holy, a sense that our fleshly finitude participates in God's infinite love. One might come to the end of a novel like *Someone* (2013) and sense something like Dante's vision near the end of *Paradiso:*

> In its profundity I saw—ingathered
> And bound by love into one single volume—
> What, in the universe, seems separate, scattered. (33.85–87)[1]

The beatific vision in Brooklyn? Yes. Dante's vision of divine coinherence offers nourishment to his fellow pilgrims, his readers. So too do the novels of Alice McDermott.

Like any good novelist, McDermott writes what she knows. Born in Brooklyn in 1953, she was raised in an Irish Catholic family and attended Catholic schools in Long Island, where she

---

1. Dante Alighieri, *Paradiso*, trans. Allen Mandelbaum (New York: Bantam, 1982).

was taught by Dominican sisters at St. Boniface and Sisters of St. Joseph at Sacred Heart Academy. (Readers who grew up in a similar setting—like the author of this essay—will marvel at the consummate, unsentimental verisimilitude with which she depicts that parochial milieu.) She has described her "requisite turning away from religion in young adulthood,"[2] her return, her gratitude for the Church's gifts, and her sadness at its failings. She writes about Catholics "because I am one, a cradle Catholic, and so I know the language and the detail"—language that "provides my often reticent characters" with the words "for the things they would otherwise be unable to express: hopes, dreams, yearnings, fears." She embraces the sacramental, "the ordinary transformed into the extraordinary, of outward signs of inward grace," and both word and sacrament "find [their] way into [her] work," lending it a liturgical valence.

In his classic *Christ and Apollo*, William F. Lynch emphasizes that a Catholic literary imagination informed by the Incarnation entails an artistic descent into the finite, the limited . . . the parochial, if you will.[3] Through a lovingly attentive descent into particularity, the artist ascends by illuminating the human condition for *any* reader from *any* place or time. McDermott herself articulates this incarnational insight:

> What makes me a Catholic writer, I think, is not that [my] characters belong to a certain church, or neighborhood or time or place. What makes me a Catholic writer is that the faith I profess contends that out of love—love—for such troubled, flawed, struggling human beings, the Creator, the First Cause, became flesh so that we, every one of us, would not perish. I am a Catholic writer because this very notion—whether it be made up

2. See Alice McDermott, "Faith and Literature," in *What About the Baby?: Some Thoughts on the Art of Fiction* (New York: Farrar, Straus and Giroux. 2021), 171. Other quotes from this paragraph are drawn from this essay.

3. See William F. Lynch, *Christ and Apollo* (Menomonee Falls, WI: Wiseblood Books, 2021).

or divinely revealed, fanciful thinking or breathtaking truth—so
astonishes me that I can't help but bring it to every story I tell.[4]

Over the course of nine novels (and a number of short stories), the loving radiance of her vision has deepened. Some of
the characters she depicts are saintly, if in surprising, unsettling
ways: Dennis Lynch in *Charming Billy* (1998), Theresa in *Child of
My Heart* (2002), Clare Keane in *After This* (2006), or Sister Jeanne
in *The Ninth Hour* (2017) come to mind, among others.[5] Within the
contours of their quotidian lives, characters like these lend their
own loving attention to others and sometimes sense that the life
of their loving Creator co-inheres with their own. McDermott
represents the drama of faith with soft echoes and undertones,
never with shouts. But even "the hard of hearing" may apprehend
her artful whisper.[6]

THE DIVINE *SOMEONE*

Among all of her fine novels, the spiritual resonance of *Someone*
sounds most clearly, at least to this reader. Consistently, the novel
suggests that our intimations of grace point to the reality of

4. Alice McDermott, "Redeemed from Death? The Faith of a Catholic
Novelist," *Commonweal*, April 22, 2013, https://www.commonwealmagazine.org
/redeemed-death.

5. After *Someone*, I recommend each of these novels to the reader of this essay.
I suggest beginning with *After This*.

6. I echo here Flannery O'Connor's famous comments about her own work:
"When you can assume that your audience holds the same beliefs you do, you can
relax and use more normal means of talking to it; when you have to assume that
it does not, then you have to make your vision apparent by shock—to the hard of
hearing you shout, and for the almost-blind you draw large and startling figures"
("The Fiction Writer and His Country," in *Mystery and Manners: Occasional Prose*
[New York: Farrar, Straus and Giroux, 1961]). In their April 22, 2013, conversation,
McDermott admits to Paul Elie that while she loves O'Connor's essays and letters,
she does not love her stories (Berkley Center, "Faith and Culture Lecture Series
featuring Paul Elie and Alice McDermott," YouTube video, May 8, 2013, https://
www.youtube.com/watch?v=5KxeYW9lEAU). For the metaphor of whispering,
see Doris Betts, "Whispering Hope," *Image* 7 (Fall 1994), http://imagejournal.org
/page/journal/articles/issue-7/betts-essays.

a divine Someone whose love creates, redeems, sustains, and sanctifies. The novel is narrated by Marie, a first-generation Irish Catholic born in Bay Ridge sometime in the late 1920s or early 1930s.[7] It is divided into three parts. Part 1 develops chronologically: Marie describes her girlhood—her family, neighbors, and, finally, her romantic heartbreak at the age of seventeen. Her older, bookish brother Gabe is ordained a priest but, after only a year, leaves the priesthood. Part 2 moves freely through time and across decades: young Marie works for seven years in the local funeral parlor and meets and marries a World War II veteran and fellow Irish Catholic, Tom Commeford. Her final reflections in part 3 are from a nursing-home bed on the eve of her death. In incantatory language, she recalls moments of coherence in her life, "yet another connection," in the words of her husband.[8] To use Bishop Barron's term, we might say that she discerns gleams of *coinherence*[9]: moments in which the loving kindness of "someone" analogically suggests the loving presence of a transcendent *Someone*, the One who offers, in McDermott's words, "gifts from someplace we can't quite define."[10]

7. This essay draws from Paul J. Contino, "Gleams of Life Everlasting in Alice McDermott's *Someone*," *Christianity and Literature* 63, no. 4 (Summer 2014): 503–511.

8. Alice McDermott, *Someone* (New York: Farrar, Straus and Giroux, 2013), 162.

9. In *The Priority of Christ: Toward a Postliberal Catholicism* (Grand Rapids, MI: Brazos, 2007), Bishop Robert Barron employs the word "coinherence" to describe the way in which God's triune loving presence grounds the human capacity to know reality. In his chapter on "The Nature of the Christ-Mind," drawing especially on St. Thomas Aquinas, he writes of "the mutual illumination of meaning of both subject and object in their coinherent act of knowing. The mystical dimension of ordinary knowing becomes clear when we recall that the mutuality between finite knower and finite known is a participation in the elemental mutuality between divine knower and creature that constitutes the very being of the creature. That is, the intellectual coinherence of God and creature—the relationality that the creature *is*—is mimicked in a real though imperfect way in the coinherence between the ordinary act of intelligence and ordinary intelligibility" (157). When I say that "Alice McDermott writes like a saint," I mean that her fiction represents "this mystical dimension of ordinary knowing" and experiencing.

10. Alice McDermott, interview with Brighde Mullins, Los Angeles Public Library, October 10, 2013.

In part I, a key moment occurs when Marie's brother Gabe tries to make sense of the unexpectedly early death of a neighborhood girl, Pegeen Chehab, whose mother was born in County Clare and whose father, evocatively, was born near Mount Lebanon in Syria. Only the day before, Pegeen had fallen on the subway and been helped up by "a very handsome man," and she expressed to little Marie "her vision of some impossible future," her faith that when she falls again (this time on purpose), the man will catch her: "'We'll see what happens then,' she said, sly and confident, her thick eyebrows raised. She swung her purse slowly, turned to move on. 'That will be something to see,' she said."[11] In fact, the next day Pegeen falls down her basement stairs and is killed. After the wake, at the dinner table, young Gabe, still in high school, reaches for the family Bible, "worn and leather bound":

> He began to read out loud. He did not read in the same clear voice he recited his poems, but softly, sitting hunched over the table, the words breaking here and there under the burden of his new, thickening voice. "Are not two sparrows sold for a small coin?" he read. "Yet not one of them falls to the ground without your Father's knowledge. Even all the hairs of your head are counted. So do not be afraid; you are worth more than many sparrows." . . .
>
> Into the silence that followed, I said, "Amadan."
>
> I said it as Pegeen had said it, ruefully, shaking my head as if speaking fondly of a troublesome child. . . . And then for good measure I said it again, into the teacup itself. "Amadan."[12]

"Amadan" is the old Irish word for "fool." For her remark, heard by her parents as a rude rebuke of Gabe's scriptural consolation, Marie receives a glass of soapy water from her mother

11. McDermott, *Someone*, 6.
12. McDermott, 25–26.

and a memorable quip from her father: "'One bishop,' [he] joked, his hand to the top of my head, 'and one little pagan. We've run the gamut with these two.'"[13]

Marie is not especially pious, but she's no more a "little pagan" than Gabe is a bishop. For one thing, she never stops attending Mass. Her vision is poor (it worsens as she later suffers from a retinal detachment and a botched cataract operation), but, as her narrative reveals, she sees glimmers of grace in her ordinary life. Her spiritual vision, her receptivity to the reality of God's sustaining love (although she wouldn't use those specific words), grows keener as she ages, as her resonant memory deepens and discerns a pattern of wholeness. We hear this most clearly in the novel's final words, as the elderly Marie describes walking slowly down the stairs of her own home, just after she has, possibly, saved the life of her broken, healing brother, and after Gabe himself, in a dream mysteriously linked to reality, has interceded to God to save the life of her firstborn son. In her final words she remembers Pegeen:

> I went down the stairs carefully in the dark, one hand on the banister, one hand on the wall. What light came from the lampposts outside the living-room window was pooled at the bottom of the stairs. I thought of Pegeen Chehab and her last fall. And then of the distance her parents had traveled to bring her to her brief life, sands of Syria and Mount Lebanon and the slick floor of the pitching [immigrant] ship, and then that brief flame in the parlor floor window.

> On the day before she died, Pegeen leaned down to me, her eyes sparkling with her plan. She said, If I see him, I'll get real close. I'll pretend to fall, see, and he'll catch me and say, Is it you again? Someone nice.

13. McDermott, 27.

She told me, poor sparrow, poor fool, We'll see what happens then.[14]

The silent white space that follows these lines—"the mystery of the silence at the end of the story"[15]—bespeaks the mystery of divine love, of an unexpected *Someone* who catches and sustains us.

SCRIPTURE, LIGHT, AND LITANY IN *SOMEONE*

The novel's final paragraphs are rich with verbal echoes, "rhymes" of images and phrases that come before, much like the recapitulations that sound at the end of Dostoevsky's *Brothers Karamazov* and bring that open-ended Christian novel to its resonant close.[16] Three reverberations especially resonate. First, the conjunction of scriptural images—sparrow, poor fool—recalls Shakespeare: Hamlet confides, "There is a special providence in the fall of a sparrow"; yet "my poor fool is hanged," keens Lear. Young Gabe's faith in God's sustaining love for the sparrow and for us and little Marie's rebuttal "Amadan" ("fool") converge, like those lines in Shakespeare. The terrible sorrow of fleshly finitude, fully experienced, opens, unexpectedly, foolishly, to the possibility of more. But that more will be fully revealed only "then" (the novel's final, promising word). Earlier, Marie had discerned an analogical image of convergence and coinherence when she observed loved ones embracing at the local airport: "Every anticipated crisis had been averted, and thus something celebratory and delightful about each ordinary reunion . . . something of the resurrection and the life all about this particular part of LaGuardia."[17] A breeze from the Holy Land, Mount Lebanon, blows through Brooklyn.

14. McDermott, 232.

15. Isak Dinesen, quoted by McDermott in "Faith and Culture Lecture Series featuring Paul Elie and Alice McDermott."

16. For my "Catholic" reading of that novel, see *Dostoevsky's Incarnational Realism: Finding Christ among the Karamazovs* (Eugene, OR: Cascade, 2020).

17. McDermott, *Someone, 146.*

Second, the image of light: the glowing lamp that appears in Pegeen's apartment suggests a luminous presence that recurs throughout the novel. Third, McDermott's repetitive rhythms of language are incantatory. As noted earlier, McDermott credits her participation in the litany that is the liturgy, the gathering that analogically points, beyond space and time, to a communal beatitude where death is no more. Keeping in mind this powerful conclusion—and the novel as a whole—*Someone* presents significant counterevidence to Paul Elie's claim that "Christian belief figures into literary fiction in our place and time as something between a dead language and a hangover."[18]

Here I will delve a bit more deeply into these three aspects— Scripture, light, litany—as they give form to the novel as a whole. Another resonant passage of Scripture is drawn from John 9. First, some context: At the age of seventeen, weeping after being jilted by Walter Hartnett, he of the wandering eye, Marie rages against her homely near-sightedness. She "raise[s] a fist against God for how He had shaped me in that first darkness: unlovely and unloved."[19] Gabe, no longer a priest, hears her weeping and suggests that they take a walk. Near its end, she pleads, "Who's going to love me?" and Gabe assures her, simply: "Someone will."[20] Just before his assurance, a young man had stopped Gabe in the street and awkwardly greeted him as "Father." This young man, a brewer worker named Tom Commeford, had taken his lunch break by attending Mass, celebrated by then-Father Gabe. Unbeknownst to near-sighted Marie, Tom will someday become her loving husband.

A few years later, at a homecoming party for World War II veterans, Marie invites Tom to her home to visit with Gabe. Tom

18. Paul Elie, "Has Fiction Lost Its Faith?" *NY Times Book Review*, December 23, 2012, http://www.nytimes.com/2012/12/23/books/review/has-fiction-lost-its-faith .html.

19. McDermott, *Someone, 79.*

20. McDermott, 88.

still remembers Gabe's sermons—especially the one about the man born blind (John 9). During his seven tedious months in a German POW camp, Tom had taken up painting. One day he spit into clay to make paint. Enacting that gesture, he remembered Gabe's sermon about the blind man. Gabe and Marie think he's referring to the neighborhood's recently deceased "blind umpire," Billy Corrigan, whom Gabe had mentioned in that sermon. But Tom "earnestly" corrects and "silence[s]" them: no, he insists, it was the story of the blind man healed by Jesus. Gabe too remembers, and Tom tells the story, "utterly delighted by yet another connection being made, between that lonely time in the prison camp and this homely one here at our dining-room table, between Gabe's words and his own":

> He looked into his palm. "And I thought about what you said, how the guy's just sitting there, not asking, not wearing himself out with asking, you said, and, bingo, Jesus cures him. Just because he feels sorry for the guy. We had lunch together. We talked about it." He looked up. "I don't know," he said cautiously. "It was a good thing to remember, over there. That you didn't necessarily have to ask. Or even believe. It gave me hope."[21]

Tom breaks the tension with a characteristically goofy pun: "And I don't mean Bob Hope." But then, with even greater intensity, he relates the story of his capture and the way he was almost killed by a bitter old German who had just lost his son in the war. Marie is "both embarrassed and dismayed to see the light [of the chandelier] reflect a sudden tear" in Tom's eye. Although put off by his "stream of talk," she feels "the unmistakable tug of sympathy for a guy who had been through so much."[22]

The recurring image of light suggests the coinherence of God's love with our own. Marie takes a job at the neighborhood

21. McDermott, 162–163.
22. McDermott, 166.

funeral parlor, and Mrs. Fagin (the undertaker's wife) and her friends serve as authors, "weav[ing] a biography of sorts for the newly dead." Their third-floor room "always seemed to [Marie] to be full of light and the aftermath of some laughter."[23] Long after their break-up, Marie meets a broken Walter Hartnett at Billy Corrigan's wake and sees him reach into his pocket—not for his flask but for the remembrance card: "Just before he rounded the corner, I saw how the light caught it, cupped in the palm of his hand."[24] And as she nears death in a nursing home, her eyesight failing, Marie's peripheral vision spies shimmering figures beside her caretaker: "Strangers, children in old-fashioned clothes, sometimes nuns in long habits or women with babies in their arms. A clean and lacy light all about them." When she describes this to her dubious children, she says impatiently, "Why do you think every mystery is just a trick of the light?"[25] Throughout the novel, the image of light suggests the mystery of love, the coinherence of someone and Someone.

At the end of this chapter, the unnamed caretaker asks that Marie call her so that he can help her get into bed:

I said, "I will," and the silence that followed told me he knew I lied. I saw the children move into the room.

"If you ask," he said softly, "you know I will do it for you. You only have to ask." And then he disappeared from what was left of my vision, because my eyes suddenly brimmed with foolish tears.

I suppose I stood then, because he caught me as I fell.[26]

23. McDermott, 121.
24. McDermott, 142.
25. McDermott, 176–177.
26. McDermott, 177.

This passage reverberates with phrases and images that run throughout the novel. The reader recalls the kind stranger who catches Pegeen when she falls in the subway and the story of Jesus' healing of the blind man, who doesn't ask to be healed yet is. The "foolish" tears that fill Marie's eyes are likely triggered by her memory of Tom, now dead for years, who himself had remembered Gabe's sermon and told that story in her dining room. "Foolish" recalls her girlish taunt of "Amadan." As she feels her body become more vulnerable, she accepts her own foolishness, perhaps recalling the first time she makes love with Tom after the near-death experience of giving birth to their first child, little Tom. The doctor warns them not to have any more children. "When he ran his fingertips over the scar that split my belly, he paused. I heard him catch his breath. 'This is foolish of us,' he whispered. I said, 'I suppose it is.'"[27] Again we see the "folly" of receiving an unexpected gift: a second son, James, follows in eleven months' time—"our Irish twins"[28]—and is followed by two daughters, Susan and Helen.

In the final pages of the novel, Marie has a terrible, terribly real dream: that her son Tom has been killed by drowning or drunk driving. Weeping, keening, she pleads for Gabe—mysterious, angelic, yet of "ordinary flesh"—to "ask": to "make it not real," to intercede that her son might be saved. She awakens. Young Tom is alive. It feels like a miracle: "I had asked and it had been given. His life restored." She is "foolishly certain that it had not been a dream at all."[29]

In 2007, I interviewed Alice McDermott for *Image* magazine. In the course of our conversation, she observed, "A real miracle is not an aberration, an intrusion, but a result of the confluence (Eudora Welty's word) of time, place, character, nature, of ordinary circumstances—a confluence that produces something

27. McDermott, 193.

28. McDermott, 214.

29. McDermott, 227–230.

remarkable, something transcendent. This is what the artist does: takes the ordinary, finite, daily stuff of our condition and shapes and reshapes it until it goes beyond itself, until it yields a larger meaning."[30] Christians profess a faith in what may seem to be an impossible miracle: our calling to participate in God's everlasting life and love. To read Alice McDermott's novels contemplatively, attentive to the graceful rhythms and rhymes of her sentences, is to sense that faith taking form in the most prosaic and parochial of settings. Her "saintly prose" can foster the reader's sense of Elijah's transcendent, whispering-like, gentle breeze.

RECOMMENDED READING

Alice McDermott. *After This.*
_____. *Charming Billy.*
_____. *Child of My Heart.*
_____. *The Ninth Hour.*
_____. *Someone.*
_____. *What About the Baby?*

Paul J. Contino is Distinguished Professor in Great Books at Seaver College, Pepperdine University, where he has been twice granted the Howard A. White Award for Teaching Excellence. In 2001 he co-edited and introduced *Bakhtin and Religion: A Feeling for Faith* (Northwestern University Press). He has published a number of essays on Fyodor Dostoevsky, as well as essays on Zhuangzi, Dante Alighieri, and Jane Austen and a number of contemporary Catholic authors such as Andre Dubus, Tobias Wolff, and Alice McDermott. His book *Dostoevsky's Incarnational Realism: Finding Christ among the Karamazovs* (Cascade, 2020) has been published in Russian translation (Academic Studies Press, 2023) and was named a finalist for both the Lilly Fellows and Christianity and Literature book awards.

30. Paul Contino and Alice McDermott, "A Conversation with Alice McDermott," *Image* 52 (Winter 2007), https://imagejournal.org/article/conversation-alice-mcdermott/.

CHAPTER TWELVE

Donna Tartt: Catholic Writing in Secular Form

Jennifer Frey

Donna Tartt is a Southern Catholic writer, one of the most critically acclaimed and commercially successful writers of her generation. Born in 1963 in Greenwood, Mississippi, she was raised by a family that loved to read and a Southern culture that embraced storytelling as an art for ordinary people.[1] She took to writing at an early age, even as she attempted—quite comically—to navigate the trappings of Southern girlhood.[2] Tartt attended the University of Mississippi, where she pledged a sorority despite being uninterested in embodying its rigid norms (e.g., she surreptitiously filled the Kappa Kappa Gamma's "Sunshine box" with quotes from Nietzsche and Sartre: "God is dead" and "Hell is other people").

During her freshman year, someone gave Willie Morris, former editor of *Harper's* and writer-in-residence at Ole Miss, one of her short stories. Willie decided that Tartt's literary genius was beyond what his own institution could address and suggested that she transfer to Bennington College, an expensive private liberal arts college in rural Vermont. She duly transferred and, like the protagonist of her first novel, studied the classics as part of a small

1. Donna Tartt, "Sleepytown: A Southern Gothic Childhood, with Codeine," *Harper's Magazine*, July 1992, https://w3.ric.edu/faculty/rpotter/temp/sleepytown.pdf.

2. Donna Tartt, "Team Spirit," *Harper's Magazine*, April 1994, https://harpers.org/archive/1994/04/team-spirit/.

clique of students who worked under an eccentric professor whose teaching methods were, shall we say, decidedly nonstandard. This is when she also began a close, working friendship with another soon-to-be-famous Gen X writer, Bret Easton Ellis.

While a student at Bennington, she began writing her debut novel, *The Secret History*. The novel was published in 1992 to both critical acclaim and commercial success. (Since its publication, it has sold over five million copies and has been translated into twenty-four languages.) Still in her twenties, Tartt seemed created in a lab for literary celebrity: an unnervingly erudite, gamine southern Catholic from Mississippi—the veritable backwater of mythical status in American letters—she was known for her hard drinking, chain smoking, and petite garçon style. She could easily have been a fixture of the New York literary scene, but she was fiercely private. Tartt only gave interviews to promote her books. Insofar as she had a public persona, it revolved around her publications. From her initial debut in 1992, she took a ten-year retreat from public life until she finally resurfaced with the publication of *The Little Friend*, only to go back into obscurity for another fourteen years, when she resurfaced for the publication of *The Goldfinch*, which won the Pulitzer Prize and the Carnegie Medal for fiction.

While everyone acknowledges that Tartt is a Roman Catholic, few critics read her as a Catholic novelist, despite the fact that she characterizes herself in precisely that way. In a rarely discussed essay, "The Spirit and Writing in a Secular World," Tartt claims that as a Catholic novelist, she faces a predicament: her chosen form is "emphatically secular."[3] Although the novel addresses the same human mysteries as theology—sin, suffering, mortality, and fate—it does so on the terms of this world. The novel does not preach, pontificate, or draw tidy conclusions from

3. Donna Tartt, "The Spirit and Writing in a Secular World," in *The Novel, Spirituality and Modern Culture: Eight Novelists Write About Their Craft and Their Context*, ed. Paul S. Fiddes (Cardiff: University of Wales Press, 2000), 25.

tight arguments; it is not a vehicle through which one imparts orthodoxies to the reader. Importantly, it leaves readers to draw their own conclusions about the complexities of life and character it lays bare. These "godless" qualities of the novel are a necessity of its "big and boisterous" form.[4] Any writer who tries to use the novel as a means of pushing theological or philosophical theses will fail, Tartt argues, to write a novel worth reading. The novelist who does not wish to discredit her own most deeply held convictions must shy away from *asserting* them through her fiction (though she does make an exception for Dostoyevsky—*somehow,* she concedes, he manages it).

While the novel is an inherently secular form, Tartt nevertheless maintains that literature is "the most spiritual and personal of the arts."[5] She means this in two senses. First, that storytelling can be a vehicle for touching on "the deepest and most serious spiritual truths—of fate and coincidence, of suffering and justice, of life and death." A novel gets to these truths through the details of plot and character rather than argument, assertion, exegesis, or oratory. The novel, she argues, is the only opportunity afforded us to *see* people and their actions clearly as they play out in the fullness of time and in the complexity of their circumstances. The novel is "an extended word-problem in morality, demonstrated in time via the agents of fate, character, cause, and effect."[6]

In a second sense, Tartt argues that storytelling "can be a way of praying when practiced in the right spirit,"[7] and this is how she thinks of herself as a Catholic novelist—not an author writing *about* the truths of her faith but an author writing *from* the promptings of the Holy Spirit. When we are drawn to a novel, she argues, we are attracted to "the spirit which created it—its likes and dislikes, its flaws as well as its strengths." The spirituality

4. Tartt, 26.
5. Tartt, 27.
6. Tartt, 37.
7. Tartt, 37.

of a novel is "subtle and indirect" because "it must be refracted through the highly impure and imperfect medium of human personality."[8]

This spirit of the writer, which moves us toward the creation of art—the muse, daimon, or inspiration—is not the same as the Holy Spirit, which moves us toward our beatitude. But there are similarities, as both are *spirit* and thus something at least partially received. Both "catch one by surprise" when one's attention is absorbed in something else. Tartt notes that for the saint and the poet alike, "inspiration often strikes hardest when one is not looking for it," and in that sense, it is "like falling in love." One must cultivate dispositions of solitude and silence to be receptive to either the Holy Spirit or the spirit of inspiration; divinity or daimon simply enters the quiet mind that is prepared to receive it. For Tartt, the impish spirit of the writer must ultimately be subsumed by the Holy Spirit, such that writing is a form of prayer and novels contain spiritual truths.[9]

Donna Tartt is a Catholic novelist because the vision and spirit animating her work has its source in her Catholic faith. But her Catholic literary sources are also easy to spot. For instance, her first novel clearly draws heavily from Evelyn Waugh's *Brideshead Revisited*; and much like Flannery O'Connor, all of her novels use violence as a means of helping her main characters to sharpen their vision and make deeper contact with reality. Her characters

---

8. Tartt, 27.

9. Here we find a deep resonance between Tartt and Jacques Maritain. Maritain argues that Christian art is defined by the spirit from which it issues: "*Inspiration* is not a mere mythological accessory. There exists a real inspiration, coming not from the Muses, but from the living God, a special movement of the natural order, by which the first Intelligence, when It pleases, gives the artist a creative movement superior to the yardstick of reason, and which uses, in super-elevating them, all the rational energies of art; and whose impulse, moreover, man is free to follow or to vitiate. This inspiration descending from God the author of nature is, as it were, a symbol of supernatural inspiration. In order for an art to arise that is Christian not only in hope but in fact, and truly liberated by grace, both forms of inspiration must be joined at its most secret source" (Maritain, *Art and Scholasticism: With Other Essays* [New York: Charles Scribner's Sons, 1954], 54.

tend to be deeply alienated from reality, and the action of grace in them tends to move them in ways that help them to see the world as it is rather than as they wish it might be.

There is something of the Southern Gothic in Tartt's works; they are violent, filled with deeply flawed and disturbing characters, and there are mysterious, supernatural elements that figure essentially in the plot but are left unexplained. Yet, like O'Connor and Percy, she is writing from a Catholic vision, such that the violence and alienation are connected to grace, sin, and the need for redemption. The point of the novel is not to make the reader feel good but to have them "recognize their own catastrophe," as Walker Percy so memorably put it. If the novelist holds a mirror up to the reader, we should not expect the reader to be flattered by what she sees. Indeed, she may need to be terrified.

Many critics of Donna Tartt, like critics of Flannery O'Connor, admire her talent as a writer but revile her supposed nihilism. They express disappointment or dismay that her characters are so alarmingly immoral and unredeemable.[10] But this is a failure of percipience, and it stems from a lack of understanding or appreciation of the Catholic vision that animates her work. This is true of all her novels, but for the sake of space, I will limit my arguments to her most popular and influential work, *The Secret History.*

The main character, Richard Papen, is an American version of Charles Ryder—a middle-class everyman who longs to belong to the more elite or rarefied class of people he meets when he goes to college, those who have traditions, history, culture, and

---

10. In one such view, novelist and critic Tara Isabella Burton writes that *The Secret History* is "suffused with such bleak nihilism that it borders on the diabolical." See her "Tartt for Tartt's Sake: *The Secret History* at 30," *Gawker,* January 20, 2022, https://www.gawker.com/culture/tartt-for-tartts-sake-the-secret-history-at-30. The original charge of immoralism goes back to James Wood, "The Glamour of Glamour," *The London Review of Books* 14, no. 22 (November 1992), https://www.lrb.co.uk/the-paper/v14/n22/james-wood/the-glamour-of-glamour.

the money that all these trappings require.[11] Richard is from Plano, California, an ugly and ahistorical town populated by drive-ins, tract homes, and strip malls. He considers his life in Plano as "expendable and disposable, like a plastic cup." On a lark, Richard applies to Hampden College, a highly selective, progressive, liberal arts college in southwestern Vermont, simply because he is transfixed by the picturesque campus scenes from the brochure that just so happens to fall out of a book one evening in his bedroom. The brochure showcases "radiant meadows, mountains vaporous in the trembling distance; leaves ankle-deep on a gusty autumn road; bonfires and fog in the valleys; cellos, dark windowpanes, snow."[12] Hampden College is everything that Plano isn't—a beautiful haven for elites untouched by utilitarian concerns. The brochure promises "a well-rounded course of study in the Humanities" that will provide him with "the raw materials of wisdom." Through several "tricks of fate," Richard finds himself there the following fall.[13] Although Richard does study classic texts at Hampden, it's not exactly the path to wisdom he was promised. First and foremost, it leads him and his friends to murder.

When Richard arrives at Hampden, he is overpowered by its beauty, "like a country from a dream."[14] He is also drawn to a mysterious and exclusive group of students who study under an eccentric classics professor named Julian Morrow. The group, known for their "cruel, mannered charm,"[15] is led by Henry Winter, an aspiring classicist; the aloof and darkly sophisticated twins Charles and Camilla Macauley; a boozy and beautiful aesthete Francis Abernathy; and finally Edmund "Bunny" Corcoran, who

---

11. Charles Ryder is the main character from Evelyn Waugh's *Brideshead Revisited*.

12. Donna Tartt, *The Secret History* (New York: Alfred A. Knopf, 1992), 11.

13. Tartt, 11.

14. Tartt, 13.

15. Tartt, 30.

sticks out as the least serious of the bunch and is somehow "re-lentlessly cheery"[16]—a regular frat boy among a clique of decadent aesthetes who spend most of their time reading ancient Greek and drinking.

To Richard, they are all "magnificent creatures"[17] who occupy a world he is only allowed to visit at their discretion. His only con-nection to them is his knowledge of ancient Greek, a knowledge he picked up at an institution they would never know: community college. Like any good American social climber, Richard manages to earn his place in this strange aristocracy. And he is happy with them—so happy that he cannot stand the thought of going back to the world of the hot asphalt and shopping malls of his youth, a world he has hidden from his newfound friends, who believe, somewhat implausibly, that he grew up among the Hollywood *nouveau riche*.

The principal attraction for Richard is not the group itself but its leader, Julian Morrow, a legendary yet enigmatic figure at Hampden College, who is famous in part for selecting his own small group of students whom he tutors exclusively for all four years. Julian does not teach in an office or a classroom but a meticulously cultivated "Lyceum" filled with flowers, teapots, oriental rugs, and porcelains. Richard is charmed by Julian—his wit, erudition, and air of mystery. He longs to breathe "the strange cold breath of the ancient world," and he is especially drawn to Julian's speeches about the sublime, divine madness, and beau-ty—"the fire of pure being."[18] Julian teaches them the Nietzschean thesis that the genius of ancient Greek civilization and culture was the balance it struck between the Apollonian and Dionysian elements of the human soul—the rational, calculating part and the darkly irrational and chaotic. He highlights the longing for beauty and the necessity of transcending the everyday world.

16. Tartt, 17.
17. Tartt, 30.
18. Tartt, 30, 40.

Julian's lectures on the theory of divine madness in Plato's *Phaedrus* and Euripides' *Bacchae* inspire Henry Winter to lead the central members of the clique to attempt their own bacchanal in search of Dionysian frenzy (notably, they leave Bunny and Richard out). Henry confesses to Richard that he wants to stop being himself and to leave behind "the cognitive mode of experience"[19]; his ultimate goal is to escape the prison of mortality and time. Tartt somewhat miraculously convinces the reader that four snobby kids in the Vermont woods were in fact possessed by a pagan god at midnight, but the bacchanal ends with a dead Vermont farmer lying down alone in a field on a cold night, with steam rising out of his open belly and with his brains smeared all over his face.

The young classicists would have been happy for this to have been the end of their experiment with *theia mania*, except Bunny finds out that his friends are more than quirky enthusiasts for the mighty dead—they've committed ritualistic murder. After unsuccessfully trying to keep Bunny in line, Henry eventually decides that they will need to murder Bunny too, as he cannot be trusted with their secret. And thus, the novel pushes along to the scene with which it begins: Bunny lying dead at the bottom of a ravine with a clean break in his neck, pushed there by his fellow classicists and supposed friends, including Richard.

No one finds out that the remaining Lyceum students are the killers besides Julian, who accidentally learns the truth after the case has been officially closed. In response, Julian leaves Hampden, abandoning his only students to an incompetent Greek tutor from a neighboring boarding school. The rest of the clique is starting to come undone: they give themselves over to drinking, have panic attacks, and begin to distrust and dislike one another. Even the inseparable twins turn on each other. The disintegration of their friendships culminates in Henry's

19. Tartt, 155.

suicide—his final attempt to realize what is noble and to achieve the immortality to which they all aspire as a group. Ultimately, however, it's clear that Henry's suicide is the opposite of wisdom or nobility. It is an attempt to escape the unpleasant reality he has created—an act of cowardice and ignorance.

In the end, only Richard has achieved any kind of self-knowledge or realistic vision—which is to say, some modicum of wisdom. From the outset, we are told that his fatal flaw (*hamartia* or sin) is his "morbid longing for the picturesque at all costs."[20] Richard, as middle-class outsider, is easily charmed by the beauty he encounters at Hampden. But in his encounters with beauty, he is not able to ascend—his soul does not take flight—toward what is eternal and unchanging: divine beauty, which is inseparable from divine logos or divine wisdom. Rather, Richard is stuck in a world of charming illusions, in part because his teacher prefers the fantastical to the real. This miseducation leads Richard to Dionysius, "the master of illusion," rather than to Christ, Wisdom incarnate; thus, eros does not find its proper object. The Dionysian spirit never leaves Henry, and it leads him to his third murder: the self-murder of suicide. Like Julian, when things become unpleasant, he simply exits. At the end of his life, Henry is "blind and unseeing"; he "lives without thinking."[21] His search for knowledge has totally missed its mark. It is only Richard who can see this. After Bunny's murder, Richard is no longer enchanted or charmed—he is able to see what they did as horrendously evil. Richard is left to suffer the reality that his friends have created. It is decidedly *not* glamorous or fantastical. It is bleak. But in its bleakness, Richard is able to enter into reality, to attempt for the first time to become an authentic self.

Henry's inability to live in reality is tied to Julian's, the only person he truly loved and looked up to. Richard is even able to see Julian in a proper light by the end. He was not a sage or good father;

20. Tartt, 7.
21. Tartt, 478, 463.

he was "a moral neutral, whose beguiling trappings concealed a being watchful, capricious, and heartless."[22] In this way, Julian is the truly Dionysian figure in the novel—essentially amoral, pitiless, and unable to love anyone but himself. He is careless with the power he has over his pupils because his affection for them is limited to the strength of their fealty. Richard comes to realize that the source of his love for Julian was his desire for fantasy over reality—for the easy charm of the picturesque over the depth of the truly beautiful. Julian romanticized, embroidered, flattered, and reinvented—he would confer "kindness, or wisdom, or bravery, or charm, on action which contained nothing of the sort."[23] What Richard ultimately loved about Julian was that he enjoyed the way that Julian made him *appear* to be. Julian was, in spite of all his high-minded talk about the sublime, ultimately content to leave his students wandering in darkness, unable to connect beauty and wisdom properly. In all the suffering that ensues, only Richard is able to achieve a clearer vision and attain a modicum of self-knowledge.

The spiritual truth that Tartt's novel communicates is that love of beauty, unless wed to reality, can be superficial and deadly. Some have read Tartt's novel as somehow cautioning against the study of the classics, but this is frankly absurd. Her novel makes little sense apart from knowledge of Plato's *Phaedrus* or Euripides's *Bacchae*; two texts that make clear, in different ways, that wisdom and self-knowledge are hard fought ends that come only to souls suitably prepared for them. While Tartt is having fun sending up her old school and some of its characters on these pages, she takes quite seriously Plato's claim that *eros* is activated by beauty, which carries within it the potential to lead to total fulfillment in the divine. What she is warning against, in a deeply Augustinian vein, is the cultivation of *misdirected* loves: she is showing us how the love of knowledge, beauty, and goodness

22. Tartt, 477.
23. Tartt, 479.

can become disordered. This occurs when we are drawn to these ends not for their own sake but for the sake of status, power, or some other aspect of our own ego. She is cautioning us against false prophets and bad teachers and being taken in by delusions of grandeur. She is also showing us what it looks like when the longing for self-transcendence and the sacred—a longing that is natural to the human soul—leads not to our fulfillment but to our downfall. If our longing for beauty is not properly ordered to its proper object, it might not be the divine that enters the receptive mind but the demonic. The bacchanal that takes place in the novel is real—and its effects are real. Henry never regrets what he did, but he also never grasps its true meaning. It is no accident that murder leads to more murder; the further they stray from true wisdom, the further they descend into the unreality of sin and evil.

The Secret History is a novel about sin, the wages of sin on the soul, and the erotic longing for knowledge, which for the Catholic is the same longing for happiness and beauty—for the possession of the fullness of truth (and goodness and beauty) in the vision of God. Our search for knowledge is only fulfilled and perfected in this final, realistic vision. When the remaining three friends meet up again at the end of the novel, it is Ash Wednesday, and they attend Mass together. They each receive the ashes of penance, but no one partakes in the Eucharist. The earlier sacred rite of the bacchanal was a forerunner to this sacred feast—but they are not yet ready for its sacred mysteries. Richard begs Camilla to marry him; she refuses, as she is still in love with the ghost of Henry. And so Richard heads back to California, "like poor Orpheus turning for a last backward glance at the ghost of his only love and in the same heartbeat losing her forever: *hinc illae lacrimae.*"[24] Each of them realizes that their love and longing will not be fulfilled by the other, but the ashes they've received are a

24. Tartt, 520.

sign of humility and self-knowledge. There is hope, for Richard in particular, that what he longs for he might find.

While some critics have claimed that Tartt does not take seriously the possibility that love of beauty can lead us to the divine, we can see that her entire novel depends upon her belief in this. What Tartt recognizes is that the love of beauty, like the love of good and the love of truth, can become profoundly disordered and disfigured. To sin is simply to miss the mark, to miss the proper target of the longing for beauty. Richard's participation in the murder of Bunny is directly related to his sin of being easily charmed, of being drawn to the "merely picturesque" rather than toward the fullness of beauty. While it is true that Tartt leaves Richard with the salutary pain of catharsis, that too is hopeful, since the ashes on his forehead are a sign of conversion—his recognition of and sorrow for his sins. And while Richard still loves Henry, he sees him more clearly now, as one who had lost his way and is unable to move freely toward his true end. And this means that Richard may be able to cultivate the dispositions to strive for beauty in a serious way, to become a true and faithful lover in time. Tartt is content to leave things there—she hints at a redemption that she does not promise her characters.

Tartt's third novel, *The Goldfinch*, revisits many of these same themes; it explores the idea that beauty can pierce the veil of perception, but only when it is wedded to reality in its full meaning, which is to know Beauty as one of the names of God, as one formal aspect of Being itself. Her art is alive to the ways that our longing for truth and beauty goes comically and tragically wrong, and yet in all our striving for transcendence, there is an expression—however it is articulated and worked out in an individual life—of the longing for immortality and the necessity to be drawn out of ourselves and to recognize our own radical incompleteness. This is the Catholic spirituality behind her secular novels, and though it is subtle and works through indirection, though it is satisfied with loose ends and unanswered questions, it is "the right spirit" in which her writing may be understood as "a form of prayer" for a fallen world in need of redemption.

RECOMMENDED READING

Jacques Maritain. *Art and Scholasticism.*
Donna Tartt. *The Goldfinch.*
_____. *The Little Friend.*
_____. *The Secret History.*
_____. "The Spirit and Writing in a Secular World."

Jennifer Frey is the inaugural Dean of the Honors College and Professor of Philosophy at the University of Tulsa. She is also a faculty fellow at the Institute for Human Ecology at the Catholic University of America and the host of a philosophy, theology, and literature podcast titled *Sacred and Profane Love.* She earned her PhD in philosophy at the University of Pittsburgh and her BA in philosophy and medieval studies (with a classics minor) at Indiana University Bloomington.

The Hidden Secret of Christian Literature

Natalia Sanmartin Fenollera

To Cristina Borges († 2023)
"They will behold a land that stretches far away."
—Isaiah 33:17

There was a time, a distant past, though not so far away as we used to think, in which the daily life and the Christian life were one in the West. During that time, men could see the wheat seed fall into the soil and hear the parable of the sower echoing in their hearts, dig on rocky ground and pull up thistles and fearfully think about the warfare that the devil fights to avoid the rising of abundant fruit out of the good land of God. Those peasants could prune the vineyard and see reflected in their work the words that Christ spoke as he walked among the sons of men, contemplate their harvest and think of the vine and the shoots and what happens to the latter when they are separated from the former.

Their wives kneaded the bread and let it grow, after hearing at Mass that the kingdom of heaven is like yeast that a woman took and mixed into about sixty pounds of flour "until all of it was leavened" (Matt. 13:33). Their kids, who scrunched up their noses with repugnance when cleaning the herds, effortlessly understood the beautiful story of the prodigal son that returns, repented and hungry, to his father's arms.

Everything in that world reminded you of a luminous truth: that between the hoe and the soil, the mill and the oven, the saw and the wood, the flour and the bread, the contemplation and the prayer, is God.

It was a woman—the French philosopher Simone Weil, in a famous essay on work published in the 1930s[1]—who opened up my eyes, for the first time, to the ancient idea that the world is a book written by God's hand and that we have the key to read it. "It would be very surprising if a church constructed by the hands of man should be full of symbols while the universe would not be infinitely full of them," she wrote.[2] It's "infinitely full," she said. They need to be read. They just need to be read.

In the industrialized Europe known by Weil, it was no longer easy to find the richness of the Gospel and the Scripture reflected daily in people's lives. The old continent had seen a succession, under the darkness of the centuries, of empires, wars, and revolutions. Many peasants, fishers, and craftsmen had abandoned their fields, fishing nets, and workshops, seeking a better life. Cities inhabited by thousands of souls engaged in factories, stores, and offices flourished. Noise, smoke, and bustle had achieved what would have seemed inconceivable centuries ago: the separation of the human heart from the contemplation of the gifts of creation, hiding away the starry sky from it and making it forget about the daily presence of God.

1. Simone Weil, "The First Condition for Dignified Work," *Church Life Journal*, April 27, 2020, https://churchlifejournal.nd.edu/articles /the-first-condition-for-dignified-work/.

2. Weil, "Dignified Work."

Simone Weil noticed this, with her inquisitive and precise way of looking, and she wondered how the people, especially the laborers and the peasants uprooted from their land, could bear an existence seemingly so empty of God. And her answer was that they needed, as well as we do, beauty. They need, she said, "that the daily substance of their lives be poetry itself," and not any poetry, but the true poetry, that eternal attribute that flows from God.[3]

"Fortunately for us, there is a reflecting property in matter. It is a mirror tarnished, clouded by our breath. It is only necessary to clean the mirror and to read the symbols that are written in matter from all eternity."[4] Weil was not only reflecting on the routine and febrile existence of the laborers; she was also thinking about the intellectual jobs, the accountants, the teachers, and the students. According to her, the sacramental symbols that weave the universe are intermediaries that help men, assisted by grace, to intuit the existence of the eternal realities. They are levers that help them lift their eyes up and search for God.

I think that the goal for literature is largely to take that sacramental universe and weave stories with it, reflecting the immutable truths written by God in the human heart. If human beings are sub-creators, as Tolkien believed; if we were given the gift of building small universes in the image and likeness of the real universe created by God; if every time writers tell us a story (with a small *s*), they are imitating the splendid and unique action of God, who weaves the Story (with a capital *S*) from eternity; then these narrators have in their hands an astonishing magic that has to be managed with true fear and trembling. "A gift of any kind," wrote Flannery O'Connor, "is a mystery in itself, something gratuitous and wholly undeserved, something whose real uses will

---

3. Weil, "Dignified Work."
4. Weil, "Dignified Work."

probably always be hidden from us."[5] She believed that art involves the breakthrough into the eternal, that the novelist writes about a world "where something is obviously lacking," a universe where showing "the general mystery of incompleteness" is necessary.[6]

Attention is the only ability of the soul that gives access to God, wrote Simone Weil. If that intuition is true, and I think it is, the mission of the Catholic writer is not, as most contemporary literature suggests, to look inside, focusing on oneself, but rather to pay attention to what is outside of oneself, gazing at the symbols with which God adorns the world to remind us that "obviously" something is missing, that this is not our home, that life is a journey, and that the signs that orient us at the crossroads are everywhere. "The Christian novelist . . . believes that the natural world contains the supernatural. . . . The novelist is required to open his eyes on the world around him and look," says Flannery O'Connor.[7]

"All good things are one thing," wrote a young and in-love G.K. Chesterton in 1899 to his future wife, Frances Blogg, in one of the most beautiful texts that I know on the sacramental nature of the world and the silent presence of God. With that extraordinary acuity that allowed him, seemingly effortlessly, to see what for most of us is hard to understand, Chesterton points out, "Sunsets, schools of philosophy, babies, constellations, cathedrals, operas, mountains, horses, poems—all these are merely disguises. One thing is always walking among us in fancy-dress, in the grey cloak of a church or the green cloak of a meadow. He is always behind, His form makes the folds fall so superbly."[8]

Attempting to reflect that mystery is, in my opinion, one of the most fascinating challenges that a writer can face, and to

5. Flannery O'Connor, *Mystery and Manners: Occasional Prose* (New York: Farrar, Straus and Giroux, 1969), 81.

6. O'Connor, 167.

7. O'Connor, 176–177.

8. G.K. Chesterton, letter to Frances Blogg, July 11, 1899, in Maisie Ward, *Gilbert Keith Chesterton* (Lanham, MD: Sheed and Ward, 2006), 99.

achieve it—even once, even if it is sensed by just one reader—constitutes a powerful reason for writing. To take it on doesn't involve claiming an evangelizing or indoctrinating task that is not the responsibility of the writer, but rather utilizing language to show not only what the natural intelligence allows us to see but also the deep meaning that the supernatural gaze provides, that gaze upon the world that looks beyond the surface, that is found under the light of faith and that operates as the fixed and eternal lighthouse that is unfazed by any storm. One of the roles of the Catholic Church, said Flannery O'Connor, is to transmit the "prophetic vision," which is valid for all times, and when the Catholic novelist "has this as a part of his own vision, he has a powerful extension of sight."[9]

Some of the writers gathered in this book have been especially conscious of the difficulty of that challenge, and they have accepted it in a thoughtful way. True fiction must necessarily handle facts, wrote Sigrid Undset, "but its chief concern must be with the truths behind the facts."[10] Undset, as well as Flannery O'Connor, was clear that the writer works with the truth. She knew very well—and it's not possible to overlook it while reading her work—that the view of the Catholic writer, conscious of those "truths behind the facts," is not limited to the natural world. His view, a view acquired in faith, sees the human race fall and be lifted up from the beginning of time; it sees man and woman leave Eden in tears; it contemplates the history of a creature that has rebelled against its Creator from the beginning of the world; it sees the wounded beauty of an earth where sin, evil, and betrayal abound, but grace superabounds. "A writer seems to see

9. O'Connor, *Mystery and Manners*, 179–180.

10. Sigrid Undset, "Truth and Fiction," *America* 67 (1942), https://www.americamagazine.org/arts-culture/2022/03/22/sigrid-undset-truth-fiction-vantage-point-242614.

in advance the gloom through which we must pass—'the dark places'—and seeks to find a way out," wrote Undset.[11]

Although each view is unique, the fact that a masculine or feminine eye, soul, and intelligence describe that reality makes an obvious difference, even though that's not the way modern culture understands it. A world only spoken by men would lack a considerable range of colors and shades, just as would happen with a world portrayed only by women. But they both have the same task: to see beyond themselves, to tell a story reflecting the order that God has created and humanity has broken, to aim to catch a glint, barely a flash, of that majesty and that misery. Is it to tell with words, as ancient people did from the beginning, the destiny of the being created in the image and likeness of God and the obstacles that must be overcome in order to fulfill in him the divine plan to which he is called. This quality possessed by literature, which does not exist in philosophy nor in the sciences, is what transforms it, in the words of John Henry Newman, into an archive of the human experience, and what makes it "the Life and Remains of the natural man, innocent or guilty."[12]

If literature is the great biographer of human history, as Newman thought, and if, as Aristotle teaches, the function of art is to imitate reality, then literature must reflect the lights and shadows, the innocence and guiltiness of our wounded and rebellious race. And, paradoxically, that is what prevents us from talking about a purely Christian literature, in the sense of a literature purified by grace, limpid, and essentially virtuous. "If Literature is to be made a study of human nature," notes Newman, "you cannot have a Christian Literature. It is a contradiction in terms to attempt a sinless Literature of sinful man."[13] Newman

11. Sigrid Undset, "War and Literature," quoted in A.H. Winsnes, *Sigrid Undset: A Study in Christian Realism*, trans. P.G. Foote (New York: Sheed and Ward, 1953), 7.

12. John Henry Newman, *The Idea of a University* (London: Longmans, 1925), 227–228.

13. Newman, 229.

CONCLUSION: THE HIDDEN SECRET OF CHRISTIAN LITERATURE

concludes what the doctrine of original sin allows us to guess: that literature will not be pure as long as the race that produces it is not renewed. "If you would in fact have a literature of saints, first of all have a nation of them."[14] Or, in other words, the only way to understand Christian literature is to assume that we will always find more sinners than saints in it and that its pages must confer an inescapable place to the human experiences of pain, the fall, and sin—and, especially, of grace.

The Christian worldview has the power to complete the author's image of the natural world through what Cardinal Newman called "the forgotten realities." Their echoes bring to our imagination the ancestral image of the blind poet, a man sitting next to a fire reeling off images and visions almost like a prophet. "The artist puts before him beauty of feature and form," notes Newman.[15] And from there he comes to what can be used as a definition of Catholic literature, which will never be a delimited and specific field, since it is nothing else but the art of telling a story just as a Catholic narrator would tell it, as only he can do it.

If the ancient Greeks depict the poet as a blind prophet, the Christian poet, touched by grace, is the blind person who opens up his eyes and begins to see. It is the vision for which Flannery O'Connor advocated, describing the storyteller as that blind man onto whom Jesus laid his hands and who, looking up, saw people that "look like trees, walking" (Mark 8:24). For Flannery, there are three great theological truths essential for the novelist: the fall, redemption, and judgment. And certainly, in that space so precisely delimited, there is room for the whole human experience: the sinner and the saint, joy and sadness, power and weakness, suffering and death—glimpses of the soul's depths, that reality closed to our eyes.

"If you were to see the beauty of the human soul," wrote St. Catherine of Siena to a priest, "I am convinced that you would

14. Newman, 231.
15. Newman, 122.

willingly suffer death a hundred times, were it possible, in order to bring a single soul to salvation."[16] The action of grace on this earth is the great secret about the world that the Catholic novelist knows; it is the invisible thread Evelyn Waugh refers to in his novel *Brideshead Revisited*, the string with which God guides us through dark valleys and desert wastelands, through wheat fields, through plains and mountains. As a monk in the Benedictine abbey of Le Barroux once explained to me, its reflection in the narratives opens windows. We see flashes that allow us to intuit that there is something else beyond the low and gray daily life that anguished Simone Weil, and to grant to literature the gift of aspiring to break into the eternal, as Flannery O'Connor argued, and of awkwardly describing—in an infinitely rough way, like a small child that draws the sun on a piece of paper—the transformative action of God.

"They will behold a land that stretches far away." The vision of the promised land, which does not belong to this world, reverberates in the prophetic voice of Isaiah as a call from eternity and awakens in the human heart a longing that nothing but God can satisfy; that has been a central theme of literature from the dawn of time. As I learned from the monks at Our Lady of Clear Creek Abbey in Oklahoma, "The history of the work that God's grace carries out in a human being, in an immortal soul, is like Homer's *Odyssey* where we can only start to narrate 'in medias res,' somewhere in the midst of the mystery action."[17]

"There are tears at the heart of things," teaches Virgil in one of the most beautiful verses of the *Aeneid*.[18] If, as Newman thought, all the ancient poets are religious, the tears at the heart of things that Aeneas evokes when he arrives in Carthage after the Trojan war and contemplates, in the temple's paintings, scenes

---

16. Raymond of Capua, *Life of Saint Catharine of Siena*, trans. Ladies of the Sacred Heart (Philadelphia: Peter F. Cunningham, 1860), 100.

17. Philip Anderson, "Confessions of a Village Atheist" (lecture, 2001).

18. Virgil, *Aeneid* 1.462.

of the fall of the city for which he fought, are the expression of that eternal longing inscribed on the world, which proclaims all the good things, the bad things, the beautiful things that hide in the human heart, and which is nothing but the inexhaustible yearning of the soul to see God.

From remote times, when the grace to discover God's footprints on this earth was granted to the Hebrews, any story, any tale, any poem capable of capturing that hidden presence in the world and making it shine, even if for an instant, we can always consider as our treasure, as part of that indefinable something that we call Christian literature.

Madrid, Holy Trinity Sunday, 2023